Henry F. Jenks

THE GOSPEL OF PAUL

BY

CHARLES CARROLL EVERETT

PROFESSOR OF THEOLOGY IN HARVARD UNIVERSITY
AND DEAN OF THE HARVARD DIVINITY SCHOOL

*" Though we, or an angel from heaven, should
preach unto you any gospel other than that which
we preached unto you, let him be anathema."*

BOSTON AND NEW YORK
HOUGHTON, MIFFLIN AND COMPANY
The Riverside Press, Cambridge
1893

The Riverside Press, Cambridge, Mass., U. S. A.
Electrotyped and Printed by H. O. Houghton & Company.

PREFACE.

In the following pages I present an interpretation of Paul's doctrine of the atonement which I believe to be new. Others, indeed, have had in their hands the clue that I have followed ; but they have speedily dropped it as of small account. When I speak of an interpretation of Paul's doctrine of the atonement, I do not mean a theory of my own of a possible scheme of atonement, to which some of Paul's words may be made to fit more or less loosely. I mean a statement which has nothing in it of my own, but which is based wholly upon an examination of the words of Paul ; these being taken in their most natural and direct signification.

I know that the announcement of the result of such an examination as " new " will excite in most the presumption of its worthlessness. Such a presumption is natural and unavoidable. If, however, in spite of this presumption, any will take the trouble to follow carefully the discussion, I can promise them a result, which, if not true, is at least interesting. The element of interest will be found in this, that here is an interpretation of Paul's words which differs so radically from the one commonly received that it might be called revolutionary, and which, if not true, yet fits the words of Paul more perfectly than that which is assumed to be true. For myself I have been delighted and surprised to see how one passage after another, that had not been thought of in the beginning, has yielded a precise and literal sense when brought into relation with the general view of Paul's teaching here presented. I know that to some this literalness and definiteness may seem petty, and the results reached may seem unromantic, compared with the generous freedom with which these words are often handled, and the sublime and mysterious significance which has been attached to them. Such pettiness, however, is the only way by which the real meaning of a writer like Paul can be reached ; and I think that the result arrived at will be seen to involve ideas which, to a man like Paul, situated as he was, were natural if not inevitable.

It has seemed to me that one great obstacle which will stand in the way of the acceptance of the view of Paul's teaching here presented will arise from the association of Paul's form of speech with ideas that have long prevailed in the church, especially with the notion that Christ in his death bore vicariously the penalty of the world's sin. I have, accordingly, judged it best, before presenting my own view, to attempt to remove these associations. The substitutionary view has rested partly upon a theory of ancient sacrifice which I believe to be erroneous, and which, indeed, is fast tending to become obsolete. For this reason I have presented in the first chapter some consideration of the nature of sacrifice. The substitutionary view has rested also, to a large degree, upon the assumed authority of the ancient church. It therefore seemed best to show in the next chapter that the history of the doctrine does not furnish a presumption of its Pauline origin, but tends to make this improbable. After this, in the third chapter, it is attempted to show, by a few illustrations, that this doctrine, in fact, cannot be reconciled with Paul's language. After this preparation, what I conceive to be the true interpre-

tation of Paul's teaching is stated and defended.
This is followed by a brief glance at the relation
of this view of Paul's theory of the atonement to
the rest of his teaching. It will be found to
throw much light upon this, especially upon his
doctrine of election.

I have not thought it worth while to consider
at great length the Socinian and other rationalistic interpretations of Paul's words. Such ration-
alizing has become of late very common. It has
arisen from the fact that the substitutionary
view has seemed contrary to fundamental principles of justice, and therefore, it has been assumed, could not have been taught by Paul. For
this reason there has been a widespread effort
of late to interpret Paul in accordance with the
moral sense of the present time. The results
have been, unhappily, for the most part very
vague, and neither very Pauline nor very ra-
tional. The reason why I have not devoted more
time to these attempts is that they have not as
yet established such associations with Paul's
words as greatly to affect the reader. At the
same time, the habit of taking Paul's expressions
loosely, the notion that he could not have meant
anything very special even by his most pointed

utterances, will, I fear, more than anything else stand in the way of a serious attempt to reach his actual thought.

The view here presented, which I believe to be Pauline, and which, while it is remote from our habits of thought, does not contradict our moral sense, may, I hope, do something to reconcile the New Testament and the conscience of the Christian world. This examination of Paul's thought was not, however, undertaken or carried on with any such object. I may say that it was not undertaken at all in the sense that I deliberately went to work to find out what Paul meant. The interpretation here presented forced itself upon me when I first began the serious reading of the New Testament, and all my subsequent study has confirmed its truth.

I have considered it a piece of rare good fortune that so many important works bearing more or less directly upon the theme of this discussion have appeared within, or just before, the time that this book has been in preparation. Of these I will name a few that have most interested me. In this country have appeared Toy's " Judaism and Christianity," Stevens' " Pauline Theology," and DuBose's " The Soteriology of the New Tes-

tament." The first of these, while it touches
only incidentally upon the work of Paul, presents
in a helpful and interesting way the intellectual
and spiritual environment in which he lived.
The two others, rejecting the traditional substitutionary theory, present theories more in accord
with the spirit of the present age. I shall refer
to them briefly in the text. Of those published
in England may be mentioned the first volume
of Smith's "Religion of the Semites," which
in certain of its aspects I am tempted to call
epoch-making; and Cave's "Scriptural Doctrine
of Sacrifice and Atonement," which in its treatment of Hebrew sacrifices is far in advance of
most works that represent the same general
position.

The Germans might appear to have been working specially for my advantage. I will name par-
ticularly Lipsius' Commentaries on the Epistle
to the Romans and on that to the Galatians, and
Schmiedel's Commentary on the Epistles to the
Corinthians, these being in the second volume
of Holzman's "Hand Commentar zum Neuen
Testament;" also the eighth edition of Meyer's
Commentary on the Romans, which is very different from former editions, having been to a

great extent reworked by Dr. Weiss, the editor.
Besides these a new edition has appeared of
Weizsäcker's "Das Apostolische Zeitalter der
Christlichen Kirche," and a new edition of Pflei-
derer's "Paulinismus," the most important spe-
cial work on this theme within my knowledge.
To these is to be added the second volume of
Beyschlag's "Neutestamentliche Theologie," in
which the teaching of Paul is made an object of
special study.

The appearance within two or at most three
years of so many books relating more or less
directly to the teaching of Paul, most of them
discussing his scheme of atonement, shows a general interest in the theme, and indicates no less
clearly the unsettled state of the public mind in
regard to the subject. Though I have differed
from all these books, so far as my special theme
is concerned, yet I have derived profit from them
all ; from some much greater than the references
to them in the text would indicate. Those that
did nothing more showed at least the views of
Paul's teaching with which mine would be confronted, and against which it should as far as
possible be guarded.

I will not attempt to name the older books

which I have found helpful. I cannot, however, pass over Weber's " System der Palästinischen Theologie," which I have found invaluable. Meyer's Commentaries have been constantly by my side, and when I have turned to Thayer's Lexicon, it has been as to a court of ultimate appeal.

The references to Meyer's Commentaries are, when it is not otherwise stated, to the American edition. The citations from the Bible are from the Revised Version.

CONTENTS.

CHAPTER I.

CHAPTER II.

THE PRESUMPTION FROM THE HISTORY OF DOCTRINE.

CHAPTER III.

THE TRADITIONAL VIEW UNSCRIPTURAL.

CHAPTER IV.

THE GOSPEL OF PAUL.

THE GOSPEL OF PAUL.

CHAPTER I.

THE PRESUMPTION FROM THE NATURE OF SACRIFICE.

I. SACRIFICES IN GENERAL.

Introductory.

IN the New Testament the death of Christ is at times spoken of as if it could be regarded as in some sense a sacrifice by which the believer is relieved from the condemnation of his sin. This use of sacrificial language in relation to the death of Christ is most common in the Epistle to the Hebrews. In the Epistles of Paul it is far less common, yet frequent enough to demand our careful attention. Indeed, there is no passage of the kind in the New Testament so important and suggestive as that which is found in the third chapter of the Epistle of Paul to the Romans. I will quote the familiar words, which may represent the general teaching of Paul in regard to this matter : —

" Being justified freely by his grace through the redemption that is in Christ Jesus : whom God set forth to be a propitiation, through faith, by his blood, to shew his righteousness, because of the passing over of the sins done aforetime, in the forbearance of God ; for the shewing, I say, of his righteousness at this present season ; that he might himself be just, and the justifier of him that hath faith in Jesus."

In this passage the death of Jesus is represented as an atoning sacrifice, through the efficacy of which the sins of the believer are remitted.   When this is said, I suppose that the thought of the majority of readers leaps to the conclusion that, in the thought of Paul, Jesus bore in man's place the penalty which the sins of the world have deserved, in the sense that his blood satisfied either the wrath or the justice of God.   Meyer's Commentary, for instance, expresses this view of the passage as follows : " For just in the blood of Christ, which God has not spared, lies the proof of his righteousness, which He has exhibited through the setting forth of Christ as an expiatory sacrifice ; that shed blood has at once satisfied his justice and demonstrated it before the whole world." [1]

[1] Meyer's *Commentary*, a. l.

This view obviously assumes that the sacrifices of the ancient world in general, and of the Hebrews in particular, had to the worshippers precisely this significance. It assumes that when, in ancient times, a victim was offered in sacrifice, it acted as a conductor to draw off the wrath or the justice of God from the worshipper to itself. If this were not the significance of sacrifice in earlier times, then this interpretation of the passage before us would clearly be without basis. The similar interpretation that is so generally given to like passages in the New Testament would also be without support. The view of the efficacy of the death of Christ which is implied in this interpretation might, indeed, be taught by other forms of speech, and we should have still to study carefully the less figurative statements of Paul and the other New Testament writers in order to learn what their thought of the death of Christ really was. If we should find that they elsewhere taught that Christ by his death did, in man's stead, satisfy either the justice or the wrath of God, then we should put this meaning into the passages in which sacrificial terms were used. This idea would, however, find no support in the sacrificial terms themselves.

It is evident, then, that, in entering upon a careful study of the teaching of Paul, it is important to ask what was the view of sacrifice taken by the ancient world. When this has been determined, we may properly turn to other forms of statement.

In the last generation, what for brevity may be called the punitive theory of sacrifice was very largely accepted. By theologians it was held, I suppose, almost universally ; with what confidence may appear from the following statement by "the moderate Bishop Burnett:"[1]

"The notion of an expiatory sacrifice which was then, when the New Testament was writ, well understood all the world over, both by Jews and Gentiles, was this : that the sin of one person was transferred on a man or a beast, who upon that was devoted or offered to God, and suffered in the room of the offending person ; and by this oblation, the punishment of the sin being laid on the sacrifice, an expiation was made for sin, and the sinner was believed to be reconciled to God."[2]

I will give another example of the same sort

[1] *Princeton Essays*, i. 323.
[2] Burnett on the Thirty-nine Articles.   Article 2.

from a German writer, also of a former generation, to whom I shall have again occasion to refer. Ernst von Lasaulx, a student of vast, though not always critical, learning in regard to classical antiquities, says in a discussion of the atoning sacrifices of the Greeks and Romans : —

" The question as to what is the sense and the original signification of sacrifice belongs to the most difficult problems of the Philosophy of Religion. History gives us no help in the matter; and language, by means of which we can in so many cases reach the underlying thought, gives us here no light. . . . We must, therefore, since nothing is given us either in language or in history, attempt to seek logically the origin of sacrifice and its original significance." [1]

This writer then goes on to explain that the origin of sacrifice was from the sense of sinfulness. He gives a vast and appalling list of the human sacrifices that have been offered ; and in these he finds the primitive idea of the rite most clearly manifested. In these, and in animal sacrifice in general, he sees the attempt to satisfy the justice of the gods. In all this he finds a

[1] Lasaulx, *Studien zum classischen Alterthum*, p. 233.

foreshadowing of the sacrifice on Golgotha.[1] He
finds a "fearful mystery" in the traces of a custom according to which the sacrificer partook of
the flesh and blood of the victim of these rites,
and especially of that of sacrificed children. This
"fearful mystery" seems to have been that in
this we have prefigured the mystical appropria-
tion by the Christian of the blood of Christ.

Nothing shows more clearly the hold that the
view which I have been illustrating has taken of
the Christian world than the fact that when the
"sacrificial theory" of the death of Christ is
spoken of even now, it generally means the vicarious bearing of the penalty which man had
incurred. I was talking with one of the most
learned and best known students of the Greek
language and literature in our country in regard
to the significance of sacrifice among the Greeks.
I asked him if, in his judgment, it was understood

[1] The essay is entitled *Die Sühnopfer der Griechen und Rö-
mer, und ihr Verhältniss zu dem Einen auf Golgotha.* It is contained in *Studien zum classischen Alterthum,* published in 1852.
I quote from this writer because in no later one have I happened
to meet so clear a statement of the position held by him; and
nowhere else have I found so full a catalogue of human sacrifices.
Probably no writer since, with anything like his learning, has defended the thesis that he maintains.

by them in the vicariously punitive sense of which I have been speaking. He replied that he had never heard the idea suggested. The possibility of raising the question surprised him. Yet at the next moment he referred to the "sacrificial theory of the death of Christ," meaning by it the vicariously punitive theory which he had never connected with sacrifice itself.

When we ask what is the real significance of the sacrifices of the ancient world, or of those that are performed by heathen at the present day, we find that this aspect of vicarious penalty is present to a very small extent, if at all.

The view that the sacrificial victim was the vicarious object of the wrath of the Divinity is hardly referred to by experts in regard to the general history of mythology and religion. The distinguished professor of Greek to whom I have just referred had never heard of it, except in relation to the death of Christ. De la Saussaye, in his "History of Religion," makes no allusion to it. It is beginning to be less generally held by theologians. The subject is, however, of such great importance in the study of the teaching of Paul that I need offer no further apology for dwelling upon it at such length as may be

necessary in order to illustrate the real significance of sacrifice. A thorough treatment of the
matter would, of course, far exceed our present
limits.

The view of sacrifice to which I have referred
was adopted, somewhat late, by the Christian
world. It appears, strangely enough, to have
grown out of the theory in regard to the efficacy
of the death of Christ which it is now used to support. This theory was adopted without any assumption as to the significance of sacrifice in the
past. In the " Cur Deus Homo " of Anselm,
the treatise that first practically introduced the
substitutionary theory of the death of Christ to
the Christian world, this is nowhere connected
with the idea of sacrifice. Later, however, by
an easy transition, naturally suggested by the
language of the New Testament, the substitutionary theory of the sacrificial death of Christ
was extended to sacrifices in general. It happened thus that a meaning which Christianity
had introduced into sacrifice was supposed to
have been derived by Christianity from the generally recognized significance of sacrificial rites.
Such reversal of relation is curious ; but not altogether without parallel in the history of belief.

When, a few paragraphs back, I introduced a quotation from Lasaulx, I did this partly to illustrate the view of which I had been speaking; but more to show that this scholar, with all his vast learning, could bring nothing to support his view but an *a priori* notion as to how men must have felt and what they must have done. There is, however, in all the departments of human study none in which *a priori* reasoning is more out of place than in the consideration of the ideas of peoples who belong to a stage of culture different from our own. The investigation into the habits of these earlier peoples has been a series of surprises. Who could have conjectured in advance anything of that widespread system of Totemism which Frazer[1] has presented with such detail, the importance of which we are only beginning to recognize, and the significance of which we are scarcely beginning to comprehend? Indeed, it is doubtful if many of these early methods of thought and action will ever be really understood, for the reason that these customs so soon become merely traditional, and those who practise them may no longer attach a definite significance to them. In looking at meth-

[1] *Totemism.*

ods of life that express feelings and notions so different from our own, we feel, so far as any comprehension is involved, almost as helpless as we do in watching the economy of an ant-hill. In the ant-hill there is a civilization very like our own, and yet, so far as the inner relations which it expresses are concerned, it is utterly foreign to us and unimaginable by us. In all these matters of early history, there is but one course to be taken : we can simply watch and compare. We must leave our own habits of thought wholly out of the account. We must take what we see without attempt at explanation, except so far as this is found in some kindred fact. In doing this, we may not reach the true explanation, but we shall escape to a great degree the danger of false explanations.

Offerings to the Gods.

In these later years, great study has been given to the mythology and to the religious rites even of the least developed peoples. There are at easy command various collections of facts relating to such themes. The admirable volumes of Tylor may serve as an example of these.

We find in such presentations a very different

state of things from that which Lasaulx imagined.
He supposed that men lived at first in grateful
trust and obedience towards God, and that while
they so lived there was no offering. After men
had sinned, they sought to atone for their wrongdoing by giving up their own lives, or by offering
other lives that should take their place. All sacrifice is of this vicarious nature. Such was the
theory. What we actually find is that the savage
recognizes forces to which he is subject, both
natural and supernatural. He is subject to his
chief. He is at the mercy also of invisible powers, and of powers which manifest themselves in
the objects of the natural world. He approaches
all these in very much the same way. Tylor
says : "As prayer is a request made to a Deity
as if he were a man, so sacrifice is a gift made to
a Deity as if he were a man." [1]

This may be illustrated by the similarity that
we find between offerings made to the spirits of
the dead and those made to the gods, or to natural objects which were supposed to be, or to be
manifestations of, divinities. This resemblance
is so striking that Herbert Spencer has used it
as an argument to prove that there were no di-

[1] *Primitive Culture*, ii. 375.

vinities except those that were, or were developed out of, spirits of the dead.[1]   The reasoning of Spencer I conceive to be, in this matter, wholly wrong, but a consideration of it does not concern us here.   It may, however, illustrate the point to which I am referring, namely, that the offerings to the gods were of the nature of those made to deceased ancestors, and that if the services to the gods had been actually developed out of funeral rites they could hardly have been other than they were, since the gifts made to the dead consist for the most part of the things which were dear in life, and which are supposed to bring pleasure, or to be of service, to the spirit in its new abode.   This being so, it can hardly be doubted that similar gifts were offered to the gods and to the spirits of nature with a similar purpose.

These offerings, in both cases, may have been made in part from love and gratitude ; but they were made most largely in order that some evil might be averted or some good obtained.   At no stage of the religious life is it quite easy to separate the elements self - interest and gratitude. Even in Christian worship it is not easy always

[1] *Principles of Sociology*, i. 257 ff.

to separate the two. In the earlier forms of religion the object of religious rites is more often to appease divinities who are ill disposed, to win the favor of the indifferent, or to preserve that of those that have shown themselves helpful, than to express pure gratitude or affection, if indeed this last purpose is ever recognized as distinct from all others. Among the early peoples, the idea of sinfulness separates itself very slowly from that of the violation of the recognized custom in civil or religious matters. With relation to the gods, sin is the conscious or unconscious offending of them, which offence is followed by the loss of their favor. Often some misfortune which befalls a man is the only reason that he has for thinking that he has offended a divinity. In this case, he may be in doubt what divinity he has offended, and thus to what divinity he shall bring his reconciling gift. Offerings of all sorts, whether of animals or of inanimate things, are gifts designed to win or to preserve the favor of the god. One cannot examine the reports of early religious customs without meeting this condition of things at every turn. Such expressions as one that is reported from the Papuan island of Tanna are very common. Here

the gods are said to be the spirits of departed
ancestors. The offering of firstfruits is accompanied by this prayer: "Compassionate Father!
Here is some food for you; eat it; be kind to
us on account of it!"[1] A good example of the
same thing is found in the following case from
Guinea. The sea was rough, and the king undertook to make it quiet for the sake of some
white visitors. He sent his fetich man with
various gifts to the sea. This representative
made a speech to the sea. "Assuring it that his
king was its friend, and loved the white men;
that they were honest fellows, and came to trade
with him for what he wanted; and that he re-
quested the sea not to be angry, nor hinder them
to land their goods; he told it that if it wanted
palm oil, his king had sent it some, and so threw
the jar with the oil into the sea, as he did, with
the same compliment, rice, corn, etc."[2] We may
place with these examples this very realistic expression in a Vedic hymn to Agni, the fire god:
"The gods eat what is sacrificed in thee."[3]

A very striking illustration of the same view

---

[1] Tylor, *Primitive Culture*, ii. 364.

[2] Tylor, *Ibid.*, ii. 377.

[3] *Rig Veda*, i. 94.

of sacrifice among a people much more advanced than any that we have thus far considered is found in one of the Hindu Upanishads. It represents a period of philosophic thought. This thought offered to the spirit wearied with the vicissitudes of the life present and of the lives to come, an eternal rest in the unconscious blessedness of the One which was the All. This result was to be reached by knowledge and meditation, and not by worship of the gods and offerings made to them. The worship of the gods was recognized, indeed, as the means by which certain minor blessings could be secured. The worshipper might win through them, for a season, a place in heaven. When, however, the power of the religious service was exhausted, the wearisome round of lower existences must begin again. Eternal blessedness or peace could be reached only by other paths. The gods, naturally enough, did not smile upon this philosophy, which would tend to draw from them their worshippers. A passage in one of the Upanishads speaks thus of one who was paying service to the gods, not understanding the deeper mystery of life : " He does not know. Like a beast he is used by the gods. As verily many beasts maintain a man, so every man maintains the gods. It is not pleasant even if only one beast be taken away. How then if many? Therefore it is not pleasant to them that men should know this." [1]

Animal Sacrifices.

The view held of animal sacrifice would seem to be the same as that of other offerings. There is in the Rig Veda a hymn describing the sacrifice of a horse, which expresses so perfectly the idea which the Vedic worshipper held of animal sacrifice that I will quote certain verses from it. It is interesting as being not only thus transparent, but as being the earliest account of animal sacrifice performed by the Indo-Germanic race.

. . . "The bright-backed horse goes to the regions of the gods. Wise poets celebrate him, and we have won a good friend for the love of the gods.

"The halter of the swift one, the heel ropes of the horse, the head ropes, the girths, the bridle, and even the grass that has been put into his mouth, — may all these which belong to thee be with the gods.

[1] *Brihad Upanishad,* i. 4, 9.

. . . "The juice that flows from thy roasted loins on the spit after thou hast been killed, may it not run on the earth or the grass; may it be given to the gods who desire it.

. . . "The cover which they stretch over the horse, and the golden ornaments, the head ropes of the horse, and the foot ropes, all these which are dear to the gods they offer to them. . . .

"May not thy dear soul burn thee while thou art coming near; may the axe not stick to thy body. May no greedy and unskilful immolator, missing with the sword, throw thy mangled limbs together. Indeed, thou diest not thus; thou sufferest not; thou goest to the gods on easy paths. . . .

"May this horse give us cattle and horses, men, progeny, and all-sustaining wealth. May Aditi keep us free from sin; may the horse of this sacrifice give us strength." [1]

I have called this hymn transparent. It shows in an extremely interesting way the double aspect under which the sacrifice was regarded. The horse was looked upon as a feast which was

---

[1] *Rig Veda*, i. 162. The extracts are taken from a translation of Max Mueller's *History of Ancient Sanskrit Literature*, p. 553.

offered to the gods, and of which they were expected to partake ; and at the same time as the gift of the animal, as such, with all his trappings, — a gift which should be for the permanent pleasure or the service of the divinities. The last verse expresses with utter frankness what the worshipper hoped to gain from the gift. It will be noticed that there is not the slightest hint of a vicarious penal aspect of the sacrifice.

This hymn may well be considered in connection with the extract from the Upanishads, which I have placed just before it. It represents the earlier and simpler form of Vedic religious thought as that represents the later and more philosophical. Both hold substantially the same view of sacrifice. In the one case, the slain horse was sent as a gift which would bring joy to the hearts of the divinities. In the later thought, it was upon the gifts of the worshippers that the gods depended for their support. Through all the intervening centuries the significance of offering to the gods had remained unchanged.

The view here taken of animal sacrifice is confirmed by the fact that vegetable offerings were sometimes substituted for this. It is obvious that if the vegetable may be used instead of the

animal, there cannot be, at least at the time when
the change is made, any radical difference in the
ideas connected with the two. Max Mueller gives
a passage from the Aitareya-brâhmana[1] which
may be used to illustrate this point : " It is said
there that the gods took man for their victim.
As he was taken, *medha* (the sacrifice or the
spirit) went out of him. It entered the horse.
Therefore the horse became the sacrificial animal. Then the gods took the horse, but as it
was taken, the *medha* went out of him. It entered the ox. Therefore the ox became the
sacrificial animal. The same happened with the
ox. Afterward the sheep, then the goat, and at
last the earth became the victim. From the earth
rice was produced, and rice was offered . . . in
lieu of the sacrificial animal."[2]

Weber truly remarks that the object of this
legend is obviously to show that the offering of
a sacrificial cake has the same efficacy as the
offering of sacrificial animals.[3] If this is so, it is

---

[1] *Ait.-br.* 6,

[2] *A History of Ancient Sanskrit Literature*, p. 419.

[3] *Zeitschrift der deutschen Morgenlandischen Gessellschaft*, xviii.
263. Max Mueller, by an arbitrary qualification, says, "For *certain* sacrifices these rice cakes were as efficient as animals."

impossible that the sacrifice of the animal carried with it any suggestion of penal substitution.[1]

The classic writers give abundant evidence of the view that was taken of animal sacrifices in the far later development of people of the general stock to which the Vedic worshippers belonged. Horace, for instance, exclaims to the fountain of Bandusia,

"Cras donaberis hædo,"[2]

precisely in the same spirit in which he cries to Venus,

" Illic plurima naribus
Duces tura."[3]

In each case it was a gift which the object of the service was expected to receive with satisfaction ; and in neither case is there any intimation of the transferrence of penalty.

Piacula.

So far as the nature of the sacrifice is concerned, there would seem to be no difference between *piacula* and other offerings. Hermann

---

[1] The substitution of the water of the animal for blood, in the Mazdean religion, is a striking example to the same effect. See p. 25.

[2] *Odes*, iii. 13.   [3] *Odes*, iv. 1.

states distinctly that, leaving out of the account a certain symbolism not concerning our present topic, "the atoning sacrifice, like every other, falls simply under the general notion of gifts with which the anthropomorphic imagination of the older humanity believed it to be necessary to support its wishes and its prayers." [1] Indeed, no such difference should be presumed unless it were distinctly stated. The ceremonies which accompanied atoning sacrifices were often opposed to any conception of them which would regard the victim as suffering, in the place of the worshipper, the effect of the divine anger. One element of these ceremonies was the dances by which the sacrifice was often accompanied. Servius states that when the Romans were suffering under the anger of the mother of the gods, and could not appease her by sacrifices nor by games, an old man danced in a prescribed manner; and he adds that this dance was the sole "*causa placationis.*" [2] And again he states that when games that were being celebrated at Rome in honor of Apollo were interrupted by the approach of Hannibal,

[1] Hermann, *Lehrbuch des gottesdienstlichen Alterthümer der Griechen*, p. 134.

[2] *Servii Commentarius in Virgilii Æneidos*, edited by H. A. Lion, iii. 279.

all the men seized their arms and rushed to meet
him. When they returned they feared that the
piaculum had failed, but they found a certain old
man dancing. He assured them that his dance
had not been at all interrupted. Hence arose a
proverb, *Salva res est, saltat senex.*[1] All this is
so foreign to our notions that it is incomprehensible. It is very obvious, however, that a service
in which dancing is at least as essential as the
slaying of the victim, and, according to the last
example, may be more efficacious than this, cannot be supposed to derive its power from the
fact that the wrath of a god has smitten a substitute for an offender.

Another indication, if such were needed, is found
in the fact that the animal offered was selected
often with special reference to the divinity to
whom the sacrifice was made. What was the relation between the divinities and these special
animals it is not necessary here to inquire. The
fact obviously implies that the divinities did, for
one reason or another, prefer certain animals to
others. They had, we might say, their tastes, although "taste" is a word altogether too superficial to express the relationship. It may have had

[1] *Servii Commentarius in Virgilii Æneidos,* viii. 110.

something to do with totemism.   However this may be, if the victim bore the penalty of the sin of the offender, we should suppose that if it varied according to any special law, it would be with reference to the nature of the sin or to that of the sinner, rather than to the divinities to whom the offering was made.   On the other hand, if the sacrifice were a gift to the divinity, the animal would naturally vary as different divinities were invoked.

The Blood of the Sacrifice.

Another illustration of the same thing is sug-gested by the use made of blood in the rites of purification.   The application of the blood of the sacrifice, when it was thus used, served to inten-sify or concentrate the expiatory effect of the sacrifice.   The most extreme example of this use of the blood is found in the Taurobolium.[1]   In this, the platform on which the victims were slaughtered was perforated.   The person offer-ing the sacrifice placed himself beneath this platform, and was thus literally bathed in the blood of the victim.   Precisely what significance the blood was assumed to possess it may be im-

[1] Vividly described in Boissier, *La Religion Romaine.*

possible for us to say. It may have been to
identify the person offering the sacrifice, so that
when the Deity looked upon him he should see
him only through the blood of the gift, and should
thus so identify him with it that the satisfaction
in the gift could not be separated from satisfaction with the giver. It may probably have been
something more profound than this. It may
have been at first, as W. Robertson Smith urges,
a means of intensifying the sense of tribal relationship between the worshipper and his god.[1]

The idea thus proposed by Dr. Smith so changes
the point of view from which sacrifices have been
regarded that it is of profound and far-reaching
interest. In itself it is clear; but the suggestions that spring from it are tantalizing in their
vagueness. It is much, however, to get the idea
that there is another side to all these matters.
When the ghosts thronged about Odysseus, what
power was in the blood, that, after drinking it,
each should speak, and speak only what was true?
Was it merely, as we might think at first, that
the blood gave them strength to speak with
earthly voice? Or did it establish some other
bond of possibility or compulsion? I think that

[1] *The Religion of the Semites.*

this latter view is forced upon us as we read, if that can be called a "view" which sees only that there is a mystery deeper than our thoughts can fairly reach.[1]

When looked upon superficially, this use of the blood has been regarded as illustrating the substitutionary nature of sacrifice. A closer examination shows that this could hardly have been the case. If the victim was to suffer the penalty which the worshipper deserved, the attempt would have been made to identify it with him. This is rarely, if ever, the case. On the other hand, the attempt to identify the worshipper with the victim is not uncommon.

However these two methods may, at the first glance, seem to resemble one another, there is really a great difference between them. The animal is identified with the worshipper in the Jewish scapegoat, for instance, where the sins of the people were laid upon his head. Among the

---

[1] An interesting illustration of this general relation is found in the fact that in the Mazdean religion the water of kine is used as a purifying agent instead of blood. This brings about, equally with the blood, some sort of relationship with the animal; and suggests that the death of the animal is merely an incidental circumstance, and is not required among people who use a different but equally efficient animal secretion. See note, p. 20.

Egyptians, the victim was sometimes marked with a seal bearing the image of a man bound and with a sword at his throat. This was to show that the victim represented the human sacrifice which milder manners had given up.[1]

If the sacrificed animal represented the giver of the sacrifice, receiving the punishment that was his due, this or some other means of identification would have been adopted. In some way or other the worshipper would have said, "Consider that this animal is I," just as, in the case spoken of by Dr. Smith, he said, "Consider this to be a human sacrifice." The use of blood of which I am speaking points in the other direction. The worshipper is not for the moment lost in the beast, thus receiving vicarious punishment for his sins. The beast is, so to speak, absorbed by the man. The man puts himself forward, smeared with the victim's blood, to make himself a sharer in the good feeling which, in some way or other, the offering had produced in the divinity.

[1] W. Robertson Smith, *The Religion of the Semites*, p. 346.

Human Sacrifices.

Human sacrifices were offered in the same spirit in which other offerings were made. Among the Aztec prayers there is one offered at the beginning of a great battle. In this the bodies and blood of those who were to be slain are spoken of as meat and drink for the gods of heaven and hades.[1] Among the Peruvians, " at one great ceremony, where children of each tribe were sacrificed to propitiate the gods, they strangled the children, first giving them to eat and drink, that they might not enter the presence of the Creator discontented and hungry." [2] These two examples exhibit the two aspects under which human sacrifices were regarded. One was the providing for the gods food of which they were especially fond; the other was the furnishing of them with persons who should in some way contribute to their satisfaction.

Of this latter the Chinese annals furnish a very good example. The emperor was dangerously ill, and his minister prayed to the ancestors of the emperor that their descendant might recover, and that he might die in his stead. His argu-

[1] Tylor, *Primitive Culture*, ii. 391.   [2] *Ibid.* p. 392.

ment was that the emperor was of the greatest
service upon the earth, while he, the minister,
being accustomed to serve, could make himself
much more useful to the imperial ancestry in
heaven than could their descendant.[1]

One indication that human sacrifices were not
of a substitutionary nature is found in the fact
that they were as often made in moments of joy
and victory as in times of disaster. In such cases,
they are obviously not sin-offerings, but thank-
offerings.

The same fact is illustrated by the circumstance
that human sacrifices were made so often to assume an air of gladness. We have seen an example of this in the case of the Peruvian children, who were to approach the gods well fed and
happy. I will quote from the ghastly collection
of Lasaulx examples to a similar effect.

At Carthage was a metallic statue of Kronos,
who stood in a bowed position, with the hands
raised and stretched out. This statue was heated
by a furnace that was placed under it. Into its
arms were placed the children that were to be
sacrificed. They fell from them into the fire beneath, dying, and with writhings which were con-

[1] *Shu King*, v. 6.

sidered to be smiles. Those who had no children
were in the habit of buying children from the
poor. The mother stood by, says Plutarch, without shedding a tear or letting a sigh be heard.
If they let a sigh or a tear be noticed, they lost
the purchase-money, though the child was sacrificed none the less Around the statue of the
god there was a great noise of flute-playing and
of tymbals, in order that no cries or lamentations
should be heard. Another author informs us that
the tears of the children were stifled through ca-
resses, " *ne flebilis hostia immoletur.*" [1]

In the same connection belongs what is related
of the Carthaginian inhabitants of Sardinia. It
is said that on special days they sacrificed to
Kronos not only the fairest prisoners, but also
their own parents, when they had passed their
seventieth year. These, since it was considered
slavish to weep, went to death with a sardonic
smile that has become proverbial.[2]

If all these sacrifices were considered as gifts
designed in some way or other to give plea-

---

[1] Lasaulx, *Studien zum classischen Alterthum*, p. 250.

[2] Lasaulx, *Ibid.*, p. 114. It is hardly necessary to say that this
theory of the origin of the term " sardonic laughter " is no longer
given.

sure to the gods, this concealment of reluctance or grief and the simulation of pleasure are easily comprehensible. If the victims were suffering the penalty of the sins of the worshippers, one would suppose that the greater the appearance of suffering the more would the wrath of the gods be satisfied.

By these examples I have designed to illustrate the fact that the fundamental notion of sacrifice was not the transferrence of penalty from the guilty worshipper to the innocent victim, but that it was the offering to the divinity of something that was conceived to be an acceptable gift.

I will quote from Professor Sayce an example taken from among the Accadians, which may show that statements that at first sight appear to bear unmistakably the significance of transferred penalty do not necessarily have this meaning. I understand Professor Sayce to give to it the vicariously penal significance. All that I would urge is that it may perfectly well be taken in another sense. "The father," it is said, "must give the life of the child for the sin of his own soul; the child's head for his head, the child's neck for his neck, the child's breast for his breast."[1] There is nothing in this, however, to imply that the offering of the child was anything different from a gift by which the anger of the divinity was bought off, and thus appeased, the head of the father being ransomed by the head of the child, his neck by its neck. Indeed, if the child were regarded as a victim of the transferred wrath of the divinity, it seems to me hardly probable that it should be taken thus piecemeal. The individual man had forfeited his life by committing the sin. If the punishment were transferred to the child, we should expect that it, as an individual, should pay the forfeit with its life. On the other hand, if the offender were buying off his forfeited life by gifts acceptable to the divinity, this purchase, part by part, seems not unnatural.

We may illustrate this by a scene in the " Rheingold " of Wagner, in which Freya was saved from the giants, to whom she had been pledged. They demanded that a wall of gold should be built, so high that it should completely conceal her, so that, looking at it, they should see not her, but the gold. Thus, in the sacrifice, the victim was so acceptable to the divinity that it concealed

---

[1] *The Hibbert Lectures*, 1837, p. 78.

the worshipper, and satisfaction with the gift took the place of anger. Perhaps the story in the later Edda which suggested this incident to Wagner may even better illustrate the matter before us. Here it was a slain otter that proved to be the son of Hreidmar which was to be completely covered with gold, so that not even a single hair could be seen. The gold concealed the murdered son. The angry father saw that, and not the result of the murderous act.

This case, in which the *corpus delicti* was covered by the gold given as a propitiation, may illustrate the idea of "covering" the sin, which was prominent in the Hebrew conception of atonement.

We may most naturally find a similar notion of sacrifice in the case which I quoted from Professor Sayce. We may suppose the father to be concealed, and his sin covered, by the child given in ransom; in the sense that when the angry divinity looked at him only the child would be seen, and at the sight of this anger would be changed to pleasure.

I must add that I know too little of the early people referred to, to express an opinion as to their ideas of sacrifice. I merely urge that the phraseology of the passage quoted does not seem to me to require the notion of formal substitution of a vicarious object of the divine wrath, or even most naturally to suggest it on a careful scrutiny of the case.

Certain Qualifications.

I have spoken as if the sacrifices were simply gifts to the gods. To this position certain qualifications are to be made. These are, however, of a nature to confirm the results which have been reached, so far as the idea of penal substitution is concerned.

I have already referred to the interesting theory put forward by W. Robertson Smith in his work entitled "The Religion of the Semites." This is to the effect that in the early history of the Semites the sacrifice was designed to refresh, or intensify, in the divinity the sense of tribal relationship. The Deity was a tribal Deity; the animal offered also belonged to the tribe. By sharing his flesh or by being smeared with his blood, the divinity and the members of the tribe were brought into fresh relationship. It would be foreign to our present purpose to discuss this view, which I understand that Dr.

Smith would extend also to non-Semitic races.
So far as it is accepted, it would obviously take
the place of the substitutionary notion of sacrifice.

Another consideration to be noticed is the fact
that religious rites tend to lose their significance,
and to become merely formal. This is what I
understand Tylor to mean by the statement that
in the development of the sacrificial idea the notion of homage to the divinity comes to take the
place of the notion of a gift.[1] An illustration of
this may be found in the manner in which the
Lord's prayer has been used as a charm, without
regard to the meaning of the petition. A similar use is made of religious literature by other
peoples, as by the Parsis, by whom it was considered a merit to have scripture read by a priest,
even in the absence of the person employing
him, and in the case of the so-called "prayer
wheels" of the Buddhists. It is possible that
in the case of the dances referred to above, those
taking part in the service could explain as little
as we the real significance or origin of the ceremony.   Indeed, the attention to the minutest
element of form in the ritual, and the sense of

[1] Tylor, *Primitive Culture*, i. 376.

peril if the smallest element were omitted or
modified, show how traditional the whole thing
had become, and how little the original significance of the service was considered. It is hardly
to be questioned that the sacrifice and the use of
blood as a means of purification came to be regarded, to some extent, in the same formal and
traditional manner. At least there must have
been a tendency to the simple perfunctory use of
such methods of winning the divine favor. Those
by whom the gods were conceived in too spiritual a fashion to admit of the earlier and grosser
notions of sacrifice might still feel obliged to
perform them according to the customary rou-
tine of worship. We are not left merely to speculation in regard to this matter. Plato, in the
" Euthyphro," represents a pious Greek of his
time trying to give an explanation of the significance of sacrifice. He gives exactly that vague
sense of obligation that I have just described.
" What is the meaning," asks Socrates, " of gifts
which are conferred by us upon the gods?"
" What else," answers Euthyphro, " but tributes
of honor, and, as I was just now saying, 'What
pleases them?'"[1] This was the faded-out view

[1] Jowett's *Dialogues of Plato* (third edition), ii. 92. The whole
passage is worth reading in this connection.

of the worshipper at the time of Plato. It is to be noticed that the earlier view which it represents must have been that of gifts, and not at all that of transferred penalty.

Pseudo-Sacrifices.

It is to be noticed that there were in the ancient world transactions which, regarded superficially, seem to be sacrifices, but which, looked at more closely, are found to be of a wholly different nature. Such a transaction was connected with the feast of the Thargelia at Athens. It was the custom that two men, taken from the refuse of the population, after having been kept for a time at the public expense, should be put to death in connection with this feast. The manner in which this was done was very striking. One of the men was held to represent the men of the city, the other the women. The one that represented the men was adorned with strings of black figs ; the one that represented the women was adorned with white figs. They were driven out of the city to the music of flutes that played an air which was reserved for this use. They were pursued by the multitude, who beat them with switches from the fig-tree which gave the name to the air to which they marched, and who, as it is sometimes said,[1] pelted them with figs and other objects. They were finally burned or cast into the sea.[2] This at first sight might seem to be of the nature of a sacrifice, and indeed it is generally spoken of as such. These men might easily be regarded as bearing the penalty of the sins of the city, and suffering the punishment which was due to all from the offended gods. One or two things, however, seem inconsistent with this view. We wonder to see them taken from the lowest class of the people, so that they are represented as giving in their appearance such an impression of wretchedness that the very name by which they were called, Φαρμἄκοί, became an expression for this sort of abjectness.[3] The manner in which they were driven out of the city does not at all suggest a sacrifice. The thing might have remained a complete mystery, if it were not for the fact that the same rite was performed at other places. In the account of its performance at Massilia the whole matter is made clear. We are told that at any time of pestilence

---

[1] Smith's *Dictionary of Greek and Roman Antiquities.*

[2] Hermann, *Lehrbuch der gottesdienstlichen Alterthümer der Griechen*, p. 415.

[3] Cf. Aristophanes, *The Frogs*, 733, etc.

the custom there was to select a poor man, to nourish him for a year at the public expense, then to adorn him with garlands and festal robes, to lead him through the city with curses, so that the evils of the whole city might fall upon him,[1] and then to cast him into the sea. The thing now becomes plain. The man was laden, not with the sins, but with the sufferings of the people. We have in a concrete form a kind of disposition of the evils of life which had long and widely been a favorite one, namely, to send them somewhere else. As far back as the time of the Atharva Veda this expedient was adopted. The Vedic singers were in the habit of sending their sicknesses and other calamities to the peoples of the mountains or other strange regions. In Horace we find an echo of the same. Speaking of Apollo, he says : —

> " Hic bellum lacrimosum, hic miseram famem
> Pestemque a populo et principe Cæsare in
> Persas atque Britannos
> Vestra motus aget prece." [2]

I suppose that the object of having the victims at the Thargelia nourished a fixed time at the

---

[1] Lion's *Servii Commentarius in Virgilii Æneidos*, iii. 57. " Ut in ipsum reciderent mala totius civitatis."

[2] *Odes*, i. 21.

public charge was that they might be thoroughly identified with the city.

We see examples of the same concrete form of accomplishing this transfer among the Hebrews, in the case of the goat that bore away the sins of the people,[1] and the bird that was supposed, so it would appear, to fly away with the leprosy of a sufferer who fulfilled the proper rites.[2] Dr. Smith speaks of an Arabian custom, according to which a widow, before remarriage, makes a bird fly away with the uncleanness of her widowhood.[3] I recall a remnant of the same idea of transferrence in my boyhood in the belief that a wart could be removed from the hand of one person to that of another. In the case of those wretches who suffered for the city, the idea is obviously that the evils with which they were laden should be burned or cast into the sea with them.

It is true that the gods often punished the innocent for the sins of the guilty. Descendants suffered for the sins of their ancestors. The city or the nation suffered often for the guilt of a citizen. One person might die for another,

---

[1] Leviticus xvi. 21.　　　　　　[2] *Ibid.*, xiv. 7.

[3] *The Religion of the Semites*, p. 402.

as in the case of Alcestis and Admetus ; but I find no reason to believe that this ever took the form of sacrifice. This rite would seem to have been regarded as a means of removing rather than of satisfying the divine wrath. It is not essential to my purpose, indeed, to insist that the vicarious penal significance was never attached to sacrifice, though this is what I believe. I merely wish to show that if this ever occurred, it happened too rarely to affect the general meaning of the rite.

II. Sacrifices among the Hebrews.

General Considerations.

I have thus considered briefly certain aspects of sacrifice in general, reserving for special consideration the ideas which were held in regard to sacrifice among the Hebrew people. Obviously, the Hebrew view of sacrifice is all that directly concerns us here. By those, however, who have maintained that the vicarious penal view of sacrificial rites prevailed among the Hebrews, it has been generally held that this was nothing exceptional, but that it was the significance of sacrifice the world over. If, however, we find that this was not the general meaning of the rite, it does not follow that it may not have been its significance among the Hebrews.

Comparative religion is, as its name implies, a science of comparison. Just so far as any one people is unlike others must the facts furnished by its history be taken into the sum of facts upon which the study of comparative religion is based. Comparative religion does nothing more than furnish a presumption with which any special religion should be approached. If this presumption, in the case of any special religion, finds itself in the presence of facts with which it is inconsistent, it must be given up.

If one is beginning the study of Buddhism, for instance, knowledge in regard to other religions furnishes the presumption that it is theistic. As soon, however, as an examination of the sacred books shows that it is in a profound sense atheistic, this presumption is to be surrendered. It is unscientific and irrational to hold, as do most popular writers upon the subject, that Buddhism is theistic because we have a right to expect it to be theistic. Science advances by willingness to give up the best supported expectation in the face of facts as truly as it does by using analogies taken from the experiences of one people to explain those of another.

If, on the other hand, in any special religion this presumption finds nothing to oppose it, then it may be safely used as at least a working hypothesis, in the attempt to explain the facts which this religion offers. It should certainly hold its own against any other explanation that is not forced upon us by the facts themselves.

To come to the case in hand, the sacrificial rites of other peoples, so far as they are known to us, are rarely, I believe never, based upon the notion that the victim bears the penalty of the worshipper, and suffers from the wrath of the divinity which is thus deflected from its original object. The overwhelming evidence of the absence of this element, so far as sacrifices in general are concerned, would lead us to assume that it did not enter into the signification of sacrifices among the Hebrews, unless the Hebrew scriptures themselves contain statements which contradict this assumption. If there were in the Old Testament a single expression that could legitimately support the hypothesis that the sacrificial victim served as a substitute, actually or symbolically, for the offerer, bearing in his stead the penalty that was his due, then this religion would be welcomed with scientific interest as offering a type of religion as unlike others in this respect as Buddhism is unlike others in respect to theism.

In point of fact, so far as the general sacrificial rites are concerned, we find no such expression. We do find, on the contrary, indications that preclude such an interpretation. Thus the study of the sacrifices of other peoples becomes an important factor in the study of the sacrifices of Hebrews.

The Fiftieth Psalm.

Among the passages that indicate the significance which was attached to sacrificial rites by the Hebrews, the fiftieth psalm is of the first importance. Occurring as it does in what may be loosely considered the central period of Hebrew history, it throws great light upon the Hebrew habits of thought. It leaves no doubt as to what were at the time the principles that were supposed to underlie sacrificial rites. The writer of the psalm represents Yahwe as angry with his people and protesting against the sacrifices that they offered him. He is represented as saying to them, —

" I will take no bullock out of thy house,
Nor he-goats out of thy folds.
For every beast of the forest is mine,
And the cattle upon a thousand hills.
I know all the fowls of the mountains :
And the wild beasts of the field are mine.
If I were hungry, I would not tell thee :
For the world is mine, and the fulness thereof.
Will I eat the flesh of bulls,
Or drink the blood of goats ? " [1]

In these verses we have presented a distinct
view of the signification of animal sacrifices; and
it is precisely in accord with the view which we
have found to be taken by other peoples. The
sacrificial victim is represented as being a gift to
God; a gift, moreover, of flesh which He is supposed to eat, and of blood which He is supposed
to drink. There is brought before us the most
interesting moment in the history of the people,
— a moment in which there was a conflict between the old and the new. The idea of the
divinity had become so spiritualized and magni-
fied that the old form of service no longer seemed
to fit Him. A kind of gift which had appeared
most appropriate to a divinity conceived of as
having limitations and needs similar to those of

[1] Psalm l. 9-13.

men, and who was considered to be in a sense
and to a certain degree dependent upon men
for the satisfaction of these needs, had become
wholly inappropriate when the divinity was considered to be a spiritual being, the Creator and
Lord of the whole earth.

We need not take this psalm as describing what
had been the significance of Hebrew sacrifice
from the beginning. There may have been a
time when, as urged by Professor W. Robertson
Smith, the sacrifice was intended to emphasize
the tribal relationship between the divinity and
his special people. This time had passed, as
Dr. Smith himself insists, at the time when
this psalm was written. It does represent, however, the view of sacrifice which had at least become the prevailing one, and which at the time
had given place to no other.

We may admit, further, that the psalm may
have put the matter in a somewhat grosser form
than was generally recognized at the time of its
composition. In an utterance of indignant protest we may expect to find exaggeration, possibly
even caricature. The sacrifices may have been
made in a vague ritualistic sense, as we have seen
was the case among the Greeks,[1] with no distinct

[1] See p. 36.

thought that Yahwe really ate the flesh or drank the blood. Making thus all possible deductions, reasonable and unreasonable, from the historical truth of the picture, certain things remain evident. One is that the view represented in the psalm was one that had prevailed among the Hebrew people. Another is that no different view had taken its place. This may have lost something of its distinctness ; but any change that had occurred must have been in the direction of such a fading out rather than of a transformation. In the light of this psalm, it is perfectly impossible that there should have been held a view so wholly different as that which regards the sacrificial victim as bearing the penalty of sin in the place of the worshipper. If this view had prevailed to any extent, the impassioned utterance of the psalm would have been wholly out of place. Even a caricature must represent, in some degree, the true outline of that to which it refers, and not present something wholly foreign and unlike. To those who believe that one view existed during the whole Hebrew history ; that the Old Testament presents at every point the same general ideas, and is never fundamentally in contradiction with itself ; to those especially who

believe that the Pentateuch was the work of
Moses, and that accordingly the book of Leviticus was completed before the Psalms were written, this psalm, taken by itself, ought to be sufficient to decide the question.

" *The Bread of God.*"

The view of sacrifices implied by the fiftieth
psalm may be further illustrated by the fact that
in certain passages in the Pentateuch the sacrificial victim is spoken of as the food, or, as the
translation puts it, the bread, of God.   One of
the most marked of these is found in the twenty-
second chapter of the book of Leviticus.   The
writer had been insisting that in the fulfilment
of vows, beeves or sheep that were without blemish should alone be accepted.   He had specified
blemishes that unfitted an animal for this use.
He proceeds : " Neither from the hand of a for-
eigner shall ye offer the bread of your God of
any of these ; because their corruption is in
them, there is a blemish in them." [1]   It is evident in this passage that the term bread, or food,
of God refers to the animals offered.

[1] Leviticus xxii. 25.   Compare also Leviticus xxi. 6, 8, 17, and
21, Numbers xxviii. 2.

In Lange's Commentary it is said of this expression, " the bread " or " the food " of God, that "it is used only of the portions of the victim burned upon the altar, and is expressly distinguished from the portion eaten by the priest. (Leviticus xxi. 22.) By a natural figure, the whole victim being food, the part of it given to Jehovah by burning upon the altar is called the food of Jehovah, and shows the communion between him and the worshipper brought about by the sacrifice." [1] This explanation could not at all apply to the passage just quoted, in which the whole animal is spoken of as the " bread of God." Indeed, the passage to which reference is made by Lange in the above extract from his Commentary tells against rather than in favor of his explanation. The passage reads, " He shall eat the bread of his God." Here, so far from a part of the food of the priest being given to the Lord, the priest partakes of the food of God. Indeed, the expression " a sweet savour unto the Lord," [2] which is so frequently used in regard to the sacrifice, expresses a similar view of the rite in a form hardly less gross.

[1] Lange's *Commentary*, Leviticus iii. 11.

[2] Numbers xv. 3, *et passim*.

The expressions "food" or "bread of God" and "a sweet savour unto the Lord," as we find them in the Old Testament, were very probably traditional ones, and I do not insist that they must be taken in their literal sense. Obviously, however, they could never have been used, if the sacrificial victim had been, or was, regarded as the vicarious victim of God's wrath.[1]

Substitutes for Animal Sacrifices.

If the sacrifice of animals had its distinctive significance in the idea that the animal suffered vicariously the punishment due to the sacrificer, it is clear that nothing could take its place. We find, in fact, such substitution in the case of the trespass offerings. The trespasses for which these offerings were made were regarded as real sins ; the sacrifices were called sin offerings ; yet in them the animal might, under certain circumstances, be replaced by flour. Thus, we read : "And it shall be, when he shall be guilty in one of these things, that he shall confess that wherein he hath sinned."[2] It is thus evident

[1] For a suggestion in regard to the Hebrew idea of the sin being covered by the sacrifice, see p. 32.

[2] Leviticus v. 5.

that the person referred to was regarded as really sinful, and as needing atonement. The first direction is that he shall bring a lamb or a kid for a sin offering. Then, if he is not able to bring a lamb, it is stated that he may bring two turtle-doves or two young pigeons. If, however, he is not able to bring two turtle-doves or two young pigeons, then "he shall bring his oblation for that wherein he hath sinned, the tenth part of an ephah of fine flour for a sin offering; he shall put no oil upon it, neither shall he put any frankincense thereon : for it is a sin offering." [1]

We have here sin offerings becoming gradually less in value according to the means of the person who had sinned. The passage is extremely instructive, for in it we have the sin offering reduced to its lowest terms. There can be no doubt that the essential element of the rite was preserved in its most attenuated form. Everything else might be dispensed with, but that which gave to the offering its efficacy could not have been left out. When as a student I attended lectures on electricity, the professor, who was a most skilful teacher, began his exposition with

[1] Leviticus v. 11.

a series of experiments with little balls of pith.
He stated that with these we saw the electrical
phenomena in their absolute simplicity without
any adventitious circumstances. The essence of
the whole thing was there, and nothing else.
The passage that I just quoted reminds me irre-
sistibly of these pith-balls. In the ephah of fine
flour we have the sin offering in its simplest and
barest form. What is obvious is that blood and
the death of a living victim are not required.
These elements have been cast aside as something foreign to the essential nature of the transaction.

In connection with this substitution of flour
for an animal, in certain sin offerings, reference
may be made to the fact that in the later Judaism sacrifices were by many held to be of small
account when compared with the study of the
law.[1] If animal sacrifices had been supposed to
remove guilt in the manner that Christian theologians have so often imagined, they would have
been so unique that nothing could have replaced
them.

[1] Weber's *System der Palästinischen Theologie*, pp. 38 ff.

The Day of Atonement.

Another passage which is extremely important in this discussion is the one that describes
the ceremonies connected with what was for-
merly known as the "scapegoat." It is too familiar to need more than a general reference.
Two goats were taken, and by lot one was selected for the Lord, and the other for the "scapegoat." That which was to be taken for the Lord
was to be killed as a sin offering for the people,
and its blood was to be sprinkled upon the mercy-
seat and before the mercy-seat. When these
and kindred ceremonies had been accomplished,
the live goat was taken. Aaron, it is said, " shall
lay both his hands upon the head of the live
goat, and confess over him all the iniquities of
the children of Israel, and all their transgressions,
even all their sins ; and he shall put them upon
the head of the goat, and shall send him away
by the hand of a man that is in readiness into
the wilderness : and the goat shall bear upon
him all their iniquities unto a solitary land." [1]

The importance of this passage for our present purpose is found in the contrast in the treat-

[1] Leviticus xvi. 21, 22.

ment of these two goats. One is offered to the
Lord as a sin offering. Not upon its head, but
upon the head of the other, all the sins of the
children of Israel were placed, and this other
was to bear them far away. It could not have
been by accident that the sins were placed upon
his head only. According to the popular view
of the transaction, the sins should have been
placed upon the head of the goat which was the
sin offering. Even Dr. Dale, in his interesting
work on the Atonement, indulges, in this matter,
in what seems to me a sort of hocus-pocus. He
rubs the heads of the two goats together, as it
were ; and when the process is completed, the
sins of the people are found adhering to them
both, or rather they have been transferred from
the head of the " scapegoat " to the goat of the
Lord. This latter pays the penalty for them by
his death. There is really nothing left for the
" scapegoat " to do but to carry away a pale and
empty *simulacrum* of the sins which, according
to the account, had been put in solid substance
upon him. Crowded out of his proper function,
he is led away, carrying only a symbol instead of
a fact to Azazel.[1]

[1] Dr. Dale's language is : " It is expressly said that the two

Dr. Cave insists that the notion, so generally
held, that the placing the hand on the head of
the sacrificial victim " signified, at every time
and in every place, the transferrence of sinfulness " is " unscriptural and contradictory." He
says : " If the victim, for example, carry the sins
of the offerer, how can that sacrifice be termed,
as it so often is, ' holy,' ' most holy ' ?   How can
its blood be sprinkled upon the altar, the dwell-
ing-place of God ?   The principal argument relied on to prove that imposition was symbolical
of the transfer of guilt is that on the Day of
Atonement the high priest laid his hand upon
the head of the goat which was not slaughtered,
thus placing upon it the sins of the people.   But
the cases are not analogous.   It is forgotten that

goats constituted the sin offering; *they cannot be severed.*   The
one is sent off into the wilderness as a visible sign that the sins
confessed over him are utterly removed, because the other has
first been put to death."

The italics are my own.   The words so marked indicate what
I have called, I hope not too irreverently, the rubbing of the
heads of the two goats together, so that the sins that were laid
upon the one should become attached to the other.   They cannot, indeed, be separated ; but, on the other hand, we have no
right to disregard the careful statements of the original, and to
confound functions between which the Bible is so careful to distinguish.

before 'this undoubted act of transferrence of
guilt,' the hand of the priest *had been already
laid* upon the head of the slaughtered goat. If
that first act of imposition — which alone paral-
leled the common sacrificial rite — signified the
transferrence of the guilt of the people, how came
it that those sins still remained upon the people,
and could be placed a second time upon the head
of the second goat?"[1] This reasoning seems to
me wholly unanswerable.

The Blood of the Sacrifice.

According to the Hebrew law, the blood was
in a special sense sacred. It must not be par-
taken of by man, for God had reserved it for himself. The reason assigned for this devotion of
the blood to divine use is, that "the life of the
flesh is in the blood."[2] It is possible that we
have in this an adaptation of sacrifice to the
more refined views of a people for whom the
sacrifice could be no longer in any gross and literal sense the "food of God." The gift was no
longer of the material elements, but of the life

[1] *The Scriptural Doctrine of Sacrifice*, by Alfred Cave, D. D.,
pp. 129, 130, note.

[2] Leviticus xvii. 11.

which manifests itself through them. Life might be an acceptable offering to the living God ; but the life could be offered only in the blood, in which in a special manner it inhered.

In the passage just quoted from Dr. Cave we see how inappropriate was the sprinkling of blood upon the altar, if the victim carried the sins of the offerer. From a wholly different point of view, Dr. Schmoller calls attention to the fact that the blood of the sacrifice was used to purify things that had committed no sin, as the altar and the vessels of the temple.[1] If the victim was efficacious because it bore the sins of man, and in his stead was smitten by God's wrath, in what sense could it be used to purify things that were by nature innocent, if even the term "innocence" can be applied to material things ?

Pseudo Sacrifices.

By pseudo-sacrifices I mean, as in the earlier part of this chapter, transactions that, superficially considered, suggest the sacrificial idea, but which are in no true sense sacrifices. Of these the following is a good example : —

[1] *Theologische Studien und Kritiken*, 1891, ii. 230. The entire article deserves careful reading.

" If one be found slain in the land which the
Lord thy God giveth thee to possess it, lying in the
field, and it be not known who hath smitten him :
then thy elders and thy judges shall come forth,
and they shall measure unto the cities which
are round about him that is slain : and it shall be,
that the city which is nearest unto the slain man,
even the elders of that city shall take an heifer
of the herd, which hath not been wrought with,
and which hath not drawn in the yoke ; and the
elders of that city shall bring down the heifer
unto a valley with running water, which is neither plowed nor sown, and shall break the heifer's neck there in the valley : and the priests
the sons of Levi shall come near ; for them the
Lord thy God hath chosen to minister unto him,
and to bless in the name of the Lord ; and according to their word shall every controversy
and every stroke be : and all the elders of that
city, who are nearest unto the slain man, shall
wash their hands over the heifer whose neck was
broken in the valley : and they shall answer and
say, Our hands have not shed this blood, neither
have our eyes seen it. Forgive, O Lord, thy people Israel, whom thou hast redeemed, and suffer

not innocent blood to remain in the midst of thy people Israel." [1]

This is obviously a civil, and not an ecclesiastical act. The heifer is killed, not by the priests, but by the elders of the people.

The later Jews, at least, had the idea of imputed righteousness. The idea of vicarious penalty was not unknown to them. [2] This relation, however, did not take the form of a sacrifice.

Perhaps nothing could show more distinctly how utterly foreign the idea of penal substitution was to the sacrificial rites than the passage which did more than any other to suggest the idea of the possibility of such substitution to the later Jews. In these familiar and pathetic words we read : —

" But he was wounded for our transgressions, he was bruised for our iniquities : the chastisement of our peace was upon him ; and with his stripes we are healed.

" All we like sheep have gone astray ; we have turned every one to his own way ; and the Lord hath laid on him the iniquity of us all.

" He was oppressed, yet he humbled himself

[1] Deuteronomy xxi. 1–8.

[2] Weber's *System der Palästinischen Theologie*, p. 313.

and opened not his mouth ; as a lamb that is led to the slaughter, and as a sheep that before her shearers is dumb ; yea, he opened not his mouth." [1]

Here we have represented a vicarious bearing of the punishment for sin ; the lamb is introduced to illustrate the patience of the sufferer. The sacrificial lamb did not, however, come into the writer's mind. It is the lamb led to slaughter and the sheep dumb before her shearers that the connection suggests. One cannot help seeing how widely the idea of sacrifice that was held by the prophet differs from that held by many modern theologians.

III. The Early Christian View of Sacrifice.

More important for our purpose than the notion which Gentile or Jew held in regard to sacrifice is the idea held by the early Christians. This is important, because as they conceived the nature of sacrifice, so they must have understood the sacrificial language of the New Testament. If they attached no idea of vicarious penalty to sacrifice in general, they would not associate such substitution with the sacrificial language of Paul.

[1] Isaiah liii. 5–7.

I have deemed this a matter worthy of special emphasis, though I shall offer but one bit of testimony in regard to it. This seems to me so clear and definite that it is in itself sufficient. The testimony that I offer is from "The Epistle to Diognetus," which is included among the writings of the Apostolic Fathers. Bishop Lightfoot believes this epistle to have been written about the year 150 A. D. The passage shows that the writer did not regard the victims sacrificed either by the Jew or the Greek as substituted objects of the divine wrath, but as gifts to the divinity. It will be seen that he takes up the matter where the writer of the Fiftieth Psalm had left it. This implies that no different view had prevailed between the two utterances. The writer had been speaking of the offerings made by the Greeks to their idols. He proceeds : —

" For whereas the Greeks, by offering these things to senseless and deaf images, make an exhibition of stupidity, the Jews, considering that they are presenting them to God, as if He were in need of them, ought in all reason to count it folly, and not religious worship. For He that made the heaven and the earth and all things

that are therein, and furnisheth us all with what
we need, cannot himself need any of these things
which He himself supplieth to them that imagine that they are giving them to him. But those
who think to perform sacrifices to Him with
blood and fat and whole burnt offerings, and to
honour him with such honours, seem to me in no
way different from those who show the same
respect towards deaf images ; for the one class
think fit to make offerings to things unable to
participate in the honour, the other class to One
who is in need of nothing." [1]

IV. Conclusion.

The object of this examination of the nature
of sacrifice and the ideas that were associated
with it in the minds of the worshippers who
made use of it, has been to determine just what
signification we should attach to the sacrificial
language of the New Testament. Before seeing
what special explanation of this phraseology the
New Testament itself offers, it is important to
understand what meaning the terms would have
apart from any such explanation. Many inter-

[1] *The Epistle to Diognetus,* section iii. The extract is taken
from the translation by Bishop Lightfoot.

esting points in connection with the general
subject have been passed over, because they do
not concern this practical result.

It is obvious, from our examination of the general theme, that when sacrificial terms are applied to the death of Christ they imply that, in
the minds of those who used them, Christ was
believed to have accomplished by his death something by which, through faith in him, men stand
in a different relation to the divine Law-giver or
to the Divine Law than they would have occu-
pied if Christ had not died.   To speak more definitely, through the death of Christ the believer
obtains remission of sins.   Precisely how this
result is accomplished the sacrificial terms do
not, taken by themselves, imply.   The significance of the sacrificial rite would seem to have
been different at different times.   It is probable
that by the later Jews it was regarded simply
as something commanded by God, and therefore
acceptable to Him.   The mere fact, then, that
remission of sins is obtained through the death
of Christ would be sufficient to justify the comparison.   Whether the death of Christ was regarded as having this power merely because God
so willed it, or whether there was in the mind of

Paul some more concrete theory of the matter by which it appeared that the death of Christ must have this power, is to be learned, if at all, from the New Testament itself.

Two ideas, however, would be excluded by the very idea of sacrifice, unless the most positive statements of the New Testament should oblige us to give to the language an interpretation that is foreign to it. One of these ideas that the terms naturally exclude is the notion that men's sins are remitted simply because, by the moral influence of the death of Christ, their characters have been changed. The other idea that the terms would naturally exclude is the notion that the sins of the Christian are remitted because Christ has borne the penalty that was his due. Both these notions are foreign to the idea of sacrifice as held by Gentile and Jew, and, as we have seen in the Epistle to Diognetus, as held by all early Christians.

CHAPTER II.

THE PRESUMPTION FROM THE HISTORY OF DOCTRINE.

Preliminary Considerations.

BESIDES the presumption in favor of the vicariously penal theory of the death of Christ that has rested on the general notion of sacrifice, there has been another and stronger presumption in its favor that was derived from the fact that this view had been so long held by the church. Though all students of the history of doctrine have known that its antiquity was not of the highest, yet it was ancient enough to be venerable and imposing. Moreover, it had been so associated with certain texts that they seemed to utter it distinctly. I will confess for myself that even after I had reached what seemed to me the true meaning of certain New Testament passages, for a while, whenever I came upon them, the traditional interpretation first suggested itself. At each time I would have to analyze them afresh, and substitute, by a conscious act, what I regarded as the true explanation in the place of the traditional one, until at last the true meaning was the only one suggested.

The authority of the past is so great, and the associations that are connected with it are so strong, that it is important to ask what this authority in the case before us really amounts to.

The question that we have to consider is, whether the circumstances under which the traditional doctrine arose and became developed to its full form were such as to give a presumption of its harmony with the teaching of the New Testament. I hope to make it appear, from the brief review which is all that is here possible, that the history of the doctrine not only suggests no presumption in favor of its Pauline origin, but that it suggests, on the contrary, the presumption that it cannot represent the thought of Paul.

The orthodox church has never doubted that the death of Christ in some way made atonement for sin. This belief has penetrated to the very heart of the Christian consciousness in every age. It is equally true that at different periods in the history of the church explanations have been given and generally accepted that were to-tally at variance with one another. To the church, the teaching of the New Testament in regard to this matter, taken, indeed, in its most abstract form and with little attention to details, has been a challenge, summoning it to the most ingenious speculation. It could not hold the doctrine of justification through Christ without attempting to give it concreteness and intelligi-bility. Thus the most widely different theories have succeeded one another, each of which has been accepted as orthodox in its time.

It is noticeable, further, that the history of the doctrine of justification has been a development of thought rather than the result of exegetical study. The idea of the atonement, taken in its abstractness, has been a stimulant to speculation. The most profound spirits in the Christian church have questioned how it could be possible. They have suggested explanations that seemed to them probable, and these have been accepted as true. These thinkers did not start out each for him-self ; each took the thought of the church as he found it. The new theory grew out of the old, either by a hardly noticeable modification of it, or by a more marked transformation. It was, thus, from the existing theory that the new thought started, and not from the teaching of the New Testament itself. I do not mean that the successive theories were not influenced by the New Testament. We see in them the effect, now of one picturesque text, and now of another. They do not, however, show evidence of a careful, or at least of a scientific, study of the New Testament, carried on in order to learn precisely what it taught.

The Apostolic Fathers.

At first the church was content to repeat in various forms the general view of an atonement. The following familiar extract from the Epistle to Diognetus is the most important expression in regard to the subject that we find in the writings of the Apostolic Fathers : —

"And when our iniquity had been fully accomplished, and it had been made perfectly manifest that punishment and death were expected as its recompense, and the season came which God had ordained, when henceforth He should manifest his goodness and power (oh, the exceeding great kindness and love of God!), He hated us not, neither rejected us, nor bore us malice, but was long-suffering and patient, and in pity for us took upon himself our sins, and himself parted with his own Son as a ransom for us, the holy for the lawless, the guileless for the evil, the just for the unjust, the incorruptible for the corruptible, the immortal for the mortal. For what else but his righteousness would have covered our sins? In whom was it possible for us lawless and ungodly men to have been justified, save only in the Son? O the sweet exchange, O the inscrutable creation, O the unexpected benefits; that the iniquity of many should be concealed in One Righteous Man, and the righteousness of One should justify many that are iniquitous." [1]

If the writer had a special theory of the atonement, this passage certainly does not express it. One thing is obvious, however, that in his mind the righteousness of Jesus is more prominent than his death. Indeed, the account of the Jewish sacrifices that I quoted a short time ago from this writer would lead us to expect that the theory of vicarious penalty would not be recognized by him.

[1] *The Epistle to Diognetus*, section ix.; from Bishop Lightfoot's *The Apostolic Fathers*.

A Ransom to the Devil.

Before the end of the second century a position was taken in regard to the death of Christ which seems to us fantastic and absurd, but which fitted perfectly the thought of the time. This view is found first in the works of Irenæus. It is to the effect that, because men had sinned, the devil had a certain right, or at least a certain apparent right, over them. From this claim of the devil came death, which Paul himself, according to Jewish usage, had spoken of as the result of sin. Jesus, the Son of God, appeared in the world in the guise of sinful flesh. The devil seized him, considering him to be his rightful prey. In this, however, he overstepped his rightful limits. Through this unjustifiable act he lost any claim that he may have seemed to possess against those that had really sinned.

An authority so revered in the church as St. Augustine presents in the most distinct manner this view of the death of Christ. After presenting the view that because the devil had slain one in whom he found nothing worthy of death, it was fitting that those whom he held as his debtors, and who believed on him that had been unjustly slain, should be set free, he exclaims, "This is what we call being justified by the blood of Christ."[1] This, he explains elsewhere, was not the only way in which men could be redeemed from the devil, but it was the best way. From the fact that the devil was conquered, not by might, but by justice, men were taught a lesson in regard to the conduct of their lives.

Petrus Lombardus presents this theory of the efficacy of the death of Christ in its most concrete form. He says that Christ set his cross as a trap, and put his blood as a bait.[2] It should be added that this view is not held with perfect consistency by this writer. In the passage from which this statement is taken, he lays stress, apparently, on the moral aspect of the death of Christ. "Satan held us," he says, "solely by the bond of our sins. These were the chains of the captives. God seized the vessels which the devil had filled with bitterness, poured out the bitterness, and filled them with sweetness." In the next section, however, he states the diabolical theory almost in the words of St. Augustine.[3]

---

[1] *De Trinitate*, xiii., xiv.

[2] *Libri Sententiarum*, Distinction iii. 19, 1.

[3] *Ibid.* 20, 1.

This theory seems to have been the one most generally accepted until the time of Anselm, who, in the eleventh century, developed a theory that was the germ of the one which later found general acceptance. Even after the time of Anselm, however, we find the diabolical theory recognized. Thomas Aquinas, for instance, in the thirteenth century, gives it a prominent place in his discussion of the doctrine of the atonement.[1]

The statements of the writers who presented this view of the death of Christ are so brief and dogmatic that they give no clue as to its origin or basis.

Two passages of Scripture occur to me that might suggest this idea. One is that in which the writer to the Hebrews says, "that through death he might bring to nought him that had the power of death, that is, the devil." [2] This passage would, however, as easily admit of two or three different explanations. The other passage that I have in mind is much more striking. It is from the Epistle to the Colossians, and is as follows : " Having put off from himself the princi-

---

[1] *Summa Theologiæ*, Part III. quæst. 49, art. 2, *et passim*.
[2] Hebrews ii. 14.

palities and the powers, he made a show of them openly, triumphing over them in it."[1]　While this passage would adapt itself in a general way to any theory of the atonement, what I have called the diabolical theory is the only one for which it has any special fitness. It certainly does not suggest the details of this theory, but the condition in which the powers of evil are left, according to the verse, is precisely that in which they are left in the theory under consideration ; if indeed it is to the powers of evil that this verse refers. It is, all along, the picturesque texts, such as this, that have done the most to shape the thought of Christendom.

Whether the verses to which I have referred did or did not suggest this theory of the efficacy of the death of Christ, it was the spirit of the age that was the most potent factor in its support. We have here an example of the manner in which the general doctrine, that by the death of Christ men are saved, has been filled out by the imagination or the reasoning of theologians, with little careful examination of the actual teaching of the New Testament in regard to the matter.

[1] Colossians ii. 15.

St. Anselm.

The theory of which I have spoken did not maintain itself without opposition ; nor, though it would seem to have been much more prominent than any other, did it stand alone.   St. Anselm gives us a picture of the unsettled state of thought in regard to this matter in his day by referring to the different views that were then held in regard to the efficacy of the death of Christ.   Those that he names are the theories that Christ by his death delivered men from their sins, from the divine anger, from hell, and from the power of the devil.[1]

Anselm may be said to be the first theologian whose reasoning in regard to the doctrine of the atonement stands in definite relation to modern thought.   With him this doctrine may be said to have commenced its regular development.   This, it should be noted, was more than a thousand years after the event occurred which he undertook to explain.

Anselm is one of the most striking figures in the history of the church, and he has exerted a wider and more prolonged influence than most

[1] *Cur Deus Homo*, Book I. 6.

theologians. His mind was a curious mixture of the sensible and the fantastic. The method of his thought was ingenious rather than logical, but his ingenuity was immense. In his so-called "ontological argument" he formed a network of fallacy which for many centuries entangled the clearest thinkers of the church, and which was broken through only by the leonine strength of Kant. In the treatise which now concerns us, his "Cur Deus Homo," we have a most curious and interesting exhibition of the man, with all the strength and the weakness of his thought. We find him manifesting the most profound sense of the divine majesty and of the enormity of sin ; we find him elaborating a theory which is imposing by its boldness, its subtilty, and its air of logical consistency. This theory he illustrates, now with solid seeming arguments, and now with fanciful conceits, which, if it were not for his grand seriousness, we should sometimes imagine to be intended for jokes, and now with suggestions which could come only from an imagination that was wholly unrestrained, and that had been stimulated by the mythology of the early church.

His argument may be briefly stated as follows :

He illustrates the awfulness of sin by saying
that, if we are told to look one way and God
says "No," better the universe perish than that
we disobey God.[1] The satisfaction for sin must
be the offering, therefore, of something that is
worth more than the universe.[2] This something
is found in the death of Christ. "Would you
slay him wittingly," asks Anselm, "to escape
the guilt of the world?" The answer is "No,"[3]
and in this way it is shown that the life of
Christ is worth more than the universe. This
great work, by which something is offered to
God worth more than all the world beside, can
be performed only by God; it is owed only by
man: thus for it there is needed the God-man.[4]

We hesitate to introduce among such solemn
and lofty thought illustrations of the other side
of Anselm's mental construction; but this is
necessary, if we are to get any true notion of
him and of his work. After recognizing the fact
of the necessity of the incarnation of one of the
persons of the Godhead, he shows that it was
the Son rather than the Father who should put
on flesh, by this illustration among others. If

[1] *Cur Deus Home,* i. 21.   [2] *Ibid.* i. 21.
[3] *Ibid.* ii. 14.   [4] *Ibid.* ii. 6.

the Father had been born into the world there
would have been two grandchildren in the Trinity.[1] The Father, born into the household of
Mary, would have been the grandchild of the
parents of Mary ; while the second person of
the Trinity, being the Son of the Father, would
be the grandson of Mary. The existence of two
grandchildren in the Trinity, he thinks, would
be, for some reason which he does not express,
unfitting. Another of the notions of Anselm is
that through the atonement God would fill out
the proper number of the angels, which had become lessened by the fall of those who sinned.[2]
The reasons that he suggests for the virginal
birth of Christ are curious and characteristic.
There are, he tells us, four ways in which human life might be produced upon the earth, — by
ordinary generation ; directly from earth, as in
the case of Adam ; directly from man, as in the
case of Eve ; and directly from woman. The
first three had been tried ; it was well now to
try the fourth.[3] Another reason given in the
same connection is, that as sin came from woman, it is well that redemption should come
from her also, lest woman despair.

[1] *Cur Deus Homo,* ii. 9.	[2] *Ibid.* i. 16 ff.	[3] *Ibid.* ii. 8.

These illustrations may suffice to show the
varied elements that characterized this very re-
markable thinker. It is important to notice
these different phases of his mind, if we would
know how far his judgment is to be accepted in
regard to any important question.

When we look at the work of Anselm as a
whole, we are struck by the fact that he also is
working over the general theory of an atonement. He is presenting his notion of an ideal
atonement rather than seeking, by a careful
study of the New Testament, to learn what is
the form under which the conception of reconciliation with God is actually taught in it. He
takes from the New Testament directly, or indi-
rectly through the church, the idea that such a
reconciliation had actually been offered ; and
then from the point which the church had
reached, he sets forth to construct the plan of
such a transaction out of his own head. So far
as his special doctrine is concerned, he does not
refer in a single instance to the authority of
Scripture. Indeed, as the title of his treatise
shows, what interested him was not so much the
development of the doctrine of the atonement
as that of the incarnation. The fact that God

had stooped to earth and had become incarnate as man, putting on the likeness of sinful flesh, was something stupendous. The question forced itself upon him, Why did God become man? " Cur Deus Homo?" There must be thought out some scheme for man's redemption which only an incarnate God could accomplish.

However imposing the theory of Anselm may be to a superficial thought, when we look at it more closely we see that it is absolutely empty and meaningless. According to the view of Anselm, Christ, by submitting himself to death, performed an act the merit of which was sufficient to balance the sin of the entire race of man. The peculiarity of the view is that this death was accepted for no object beyond itself. Anselm distinctly repudiated the view which had been so widely held, that the death of Christ delivered man from the power of the devil. His theory had not developed itself to the thought that Christ stood in the place of the sinner and freed him from the wrath of God by bearing the penalty which man deserved. Either of these thoughts would give a motive for the death of Christ, and would show how his dying for a definite end could properly be reckoned as in the

highest degree meritorious. In the theory of
Anselm, Christ, the second person of the Trinity, descended from heaven simply that he might
suffer death and return thither again. As I have
said, the whole transaction is without significance.

Thomas Aquinas.

Before considering the form in which the
thought of Anselm later received its much-
needed completion, we will notice for a moment
how chaotic the theory of the Atonement remained for some time after the work of Anselm.
Thomas Aquinas presents it under the most varied forms. At one moment the death of Christ
is symbolic. At another it is fitted to furnish
to man both an example and a stimulus. At
another we have repeated in its old form the
story of the transaction with the devil. Then
again we have indicated the solidarity of humanity. Christ can redeem men because he is the
head and they the members of the same body.
Then the death of Christ is an acceptable sacrifice. Again it is a superabundant satisfaction,
thus taking away *reatum pœnæ.* All these
conceptions are brought together without any
attempt to harmonize them or to reduce them to

any common principle. It is simply recognized that the death of Christ was effective by all these methods.[1]

Luther.

It would seem as if the theory of Anselm must by an inner necessity have become in time filled out with the penal substitutionary notion of the death of Christ. The change was helped, if it was not actually motived, by a text scarcely less picturesque than that which may have suggested the theory of the discomfiture of the devil. " Christ," says Paul, "redeemed us from the curse of the law, having become a curse for us ; for it is written, ' Cursed is every one that hangeth on a tree.' "[2] At this point the development of the theory touches, or is touched by, the language of the New Testament. It takes, however, single suggestions from single passages, and is not the result of a careful study of the New Testament as a whole, although Luther in his elaborate Commentaries made such a study.

It is worth while to notice how picturesquely Luther, in his Commentary, treats the passage just quoted, which naturally lends itself to such

---

[1] See *Summa Theologiæ*, Part III.   Quæst. 46 and 49.

[2] Galatians iii. 13.

use. " For Christ, so far as concerns his person, is indeed innocent, and ought not to hang on the cross and become a curse ; but because, according to the law, every murderer should be hung, Christ, according to the law of Moses, must hang ; for he has taken upon himself the person of a sinner and murderer ; yes, not of one alone, but of all sinners and murderers in a heap ; for we are all together sinners and murderers (for whoso is angry with his neighbor or hates him is a murderer), and therefore deserve death and damnation. But Christ has taken upon himself the sins of all of us, and has died for them on the cross. Therefore was he obliged to become what we are, namely, a sinner, murderer, transgressor, etc. Therefore Isaiah says that he is reckoned among the murderers. And indeed all the prophets have foreseen that Christ would be the greatest sinner, whose like was never witnessed upon the earth. For since he is a sacrifice for the sin of the whole world, he is not such an one as is innocent and without sin, is not the Son of God in glory ; but a sinner is he for a little while forsaken of God, who bears and has lying on his neck the sin of St. Paul, who was a blasphemer, persecutor, and scoffer ; of St. Peter, who denied

Christ ; also of David, who was an adulterer and murderer and caused the name of God to be blasphemed among the Gentiles. In a word, he is the one who bears on his body and has loaded upon him all the sins of all men in the whole world, who have ever been, are now, and shall be. Not so that he himself has committed such sins, but that he has taken them from us who have committed them, upon his own body, and that he has atoned for them with his own blood. . . . God sent his only begotten Son into the world, threw upon him all the sins of all men, and thus spake to him : Be thou Peter who denied ; Paul, who persecuted, blasphemed, and used all violence ; David, who committed adultery ; also the sinner who ate the apple in Paradise ; the murderer who hung upon the cross. In a word, thou shalt be what all men are, as if thou alone hadst committed the sins of all men ; therefore think now how you will pay and make satisfaction for them."

Since Christ by his death performed this great service for men, bearing the penalty of all the sins that ever were or ever will be in the world, the act acquires meaning and infinite worth. The willingness thus to die for men might well be regarded as an act of merit sufficient, when it is imputed to his followers, to make actually acceptable to God those whom his death had freed from the terrors of the divine wrath. The theory of Anselm thus received its needed content and complement ; and the theologian might well rejoice in this solid and well-rounded conception of the doctrine of the atonement.

Socinus and Grotius.

The development of Christian doctrine can, however, no more reach a position of absolute rest than can the development of philosophic thought. An inner dialectic drives it on. The peace of the orthodox theologian, rejoicing in his completed work, was rudely broken in upon by heretical questioning. To Socinus the result which we have just contemplated seemed not at all satisfactory. He urged, as Duns Scotus had urged before him, that Christ had made no infinite atonement, for it was the man, not the God, who suffered and died. Further, he urged that if Christ had paid the complete penalty for all the sins of the world, then God had no further claim upon men ; and, live as they might, all men had a right to heaven. If some one has

completely paid my debt, the creditor can insist
on nothing further ; and for him to make conditions would be impertinent.   Such flaws did the
awakened thought of the age find in a scheme
that had seemed so perfect.

Here occurred what was, perhaps, the most
brilliant strategetic movement that was ever accomplished in the history of theological polemics.
In the presence of the sharp attack that has been
referred to, Grotius, assuming the direction of
the orthodox defence, effected a change of front
which left almost powerless the attack that had
seemed so irresistible.   Christ, he urged, has indeed made satisfaction for the sin of the world.
But the very term implies that what was given
was not the absolute equivalent of that which
might have been required.   If I owe a hundred
dollars, and a man pays on my behalf a hundred
dollars to my creditor, he is not said to make
satisfaction ; he has paid the debt.   The satisfaction, not being the whole amount that was
due, may be whatever the creditor is pleased to
accept.   It was not necessary that Christ should
bear the full penalty for the sins of the world.
It was only necessary that God should accept
what he actually suffered in the place of the
penalty which the sinner had incurred.

It is obvious that to the doctrine of the atonement as thus stated, the objections urged by the
Socinians lose, to a great extent, their force. Since
the full price was not paid, but a partial payment
was accepted in its stead, no one has any right
to claim the advantage of it for himself. God
may impose what terms He will as the condition
upon which forgiveness is granted. Moreover, it
is real forgiveness that is granted; that is, only
a part of the debt is paid; the rest is forgiven.

Another aspect of the theory of Grotius is of
great interest as showing the manner in which
theology is affected by the changing sentiment
of the world. In every age, theology reflects
more or less perfectly the spirit of the time. It
may, indeed, very often be in arrears ; but it follows even when it does not keep pace. With
Anselm, sin was an offence against the divine
majesty. It was the honor of God that was at
stake. If God's honor did not suffer from sin,
it was simply because sin was punished. " Suppose," he said, " an object under the sky to strive
to flee from under the sky ; it flees from one part
of the heavens only to draw near to another part
of them. So if one wishes to flee from under
the commanding will of God, he rushes beneath

his punishing will.'' [1] It was not consistent with the divine honor to remit the penalties of sin, unless by an offering, like that made by the divine man, the claims of the divine honor have been satisfied.

At the time in which Anselm wrote, all this seemed very reasonable. It appeared, doubtless, to be an extremely natural and common-sense view, compared with the somewhat fantastic doctrine of the transaction with the devil which it was slowly to supersede. At that time, as long after, the people were considered to exist for the sake of the ruler. The king was the owner of the kingdom, and managed it for his own advantage and glory. If his subjects were cared for, it was rather on account of his own magnanimity than on account of any right that they had to be so regarded. At the time of Grotius, however, the modern notion of the relation between the governor and the governed had begun to make itself recognized. The people in these later days are seen to have rights which the ruler must respect. Government is felt to be for the sake of the governed, not for the sake of the governor. The ideal towards which this notion tends is that

[1] *Cur Deus Homo*, i. 15.

of "a government of the people, for the people, by the people." This ideal is far from being fulfilled, even in our time and nation. At the time of Grotius it was by no means recognized even as an ideal. We see, however, the great change that the thought of men had undergone in regard to this matter, from the fact that it was no longer the honor of the emperor of the universe that was to be guarded; it was the dignity of the law that was to be maintained. If the law could be violated with impunity, it would become degraded and powerless. Christ, by his death, did enough to satisfy the dignity and authority of the law; and thus sinners who complied with the conditions that had been established might be forgiven.

It is easy to understand why this theory, which recognized the importance of maintaining the dignity and authority of the law instead of guarding the honor of a personal ruler, should have had such an attraction for the theologians of New England.

Baur, I conceive, was wrong in insisting that in all this Grotius surrendered the ground to the Socinians, whom he fancied he was conquering. The thought of Baur is, that since the object of

the death of Christ was to make men honor the
law even while its penalties were in part relaxed,
he, as truly as the Socinians, placed the efficacy
of this death in its effect upon the minds of
men.   In the thought of Anselm and his followers, the death of Christ worked Godwards.
In the theory of Grotius and of the Socinians, it
worked manwards.   This criticism is not wholly
true.   The element of the atonement as affected
by the death of Christ, according to the thought
of Grotius, was that by it God manifested his
displeasure at sin.   The manifestation of displeasure is not made merely for the sake of being
seen.   Displeasure seeks its own manifestation
in part for its own sake.   There could be no displeasure at sin manifested if none existed.   When
a group of men have been guilty of some murderous act, and a part are sentenced to death and
a part receive milder treatment, I think the general feeling is not merely that on account of the
infliction of the death penalty in some cases,
others who are more disposed to commit the
crime will be deterred ; but that a certain respect has been actually shown to the law itself.
Thus, I conceive that in the governmental theory
of the atonement it was felt that the law was to

a certain extent honored by the death of Christ ;
and we may assume that it would be in accordance with this theory to say that God could not
bring himself to forgive sin until His sense of
condemnation had been satisfied. Even, however, if we leave this out of the account as possibly forcing an expression used by Grotius, still
his theory and that of the Socinians remain wide
apart. They may belong to the same genus, but
they represent very different species. In the case
of the Socinians the death of Christ was designed
to manifest the love of God, and thus to move
the hearts of men to an answering love. In the
thought of Grotius it was to manifest not only
the love but the justice of God, and to exalt the
authority and dignity of the law even above that
of love.

Modern Developments of Doctrine.

The manner in which the development of doctrine has taken place by a law of its own, and
with little reference to the precise language of
the New Testament, may be further illustrated
by what has been going on in these later times.
In these we have doctrine in its making ; or rather
we have doctrines in their struggle for existence.

The moral sense of many theologians has been dissatisfied with the traditional dogma of the atonement, and one and another has tried to re-work or re-state the doctrine in such a way as to commend it to the conscience of the present day. These attempts have started from the general idea that somehow Christ made atonement; and they have sought to devise a scheme of atonement that should be free from the objections that had been brought against the old. These attempts have been, however, wholly individual, in the sense that they make little claim to a Scriptural basis, and rest only upon the authority of the theologians who have proposed them, and upon that of their own merits.

One of the most interesting of such attempts was made by Dr. John McLeod Campbell. In his treatise he quotes President Edwards, who, in contending "that sin must be punished with an infinite penalty," said: "God could not be just to himself without this vindication, unless there could be such a thing as a repentance, humiliation, and sorrow for this (that is, for sin) proportionate to the greatness of the majesty despised." [1] In the thought of Campbell this "hu-

---

[1] Campbell's *The Nature of the Atonement*, p. 137. Compare Edwards's *Satisfaction for Sin*, ch. ii. 1–3.

miliation and sorrow" for sin was accomplished
by Jesus. He uttered from the depth of humanity an "amen" to God's condemnation of the
sin of man. Through this response of Jesus on
behalf of men, they are in a position to win forgiveness and acceptance with God.

The theory of Dorner is very much like that
of Campbell. According to this, Christ identifies himself by sympathy with men, feels their
sin and the righteousness of God's anger. He
gives up everything but love, and bears by sympathy even the sense of the divine wrath. "He
wraps men in by the might of his love, so that
he will answer for them, and by this substitution
of himself will save and cover them. In this
willing surrender he lets his blood flow, and
burying himself in the feeling of our ill deserts
and of God's righteous displeasure (which breaks
his heart), he gives his spirit into the Father's
hands."[1] Again, he says, "As he could not be
thought of without his humanity, so humanity
could not be thought of truly without him ; and
thus in him the race atoned for its sin."[2]

Dr. Bushnell, after having in an earlier work
presented merely the moral aspect of the atone-

[1] Dorner, *Christliche Glaubenslehre,* ii. 650.   [2] *Ibid.* p. 652.

ment, showing how the suffering of Christ was fitted to affect the hearts of men, finds at last the significance of the suffering of Christ in the fact that one cannot really forgive sin till he has suffered for the sinner.[1]

Dr. Newman Smyth presents a somewhat similar view in the statement that God cannot forgive " without condemning sin in sorrow for it." God, however, cannot suffer in himself, but only in some outgoing from himself, that is in Christ.[2]

The view advanced by Professor Stevens belongs also to the group which we are here considering. He, indeed, disclaims any Pauline authority for his special view. He says : " The question, Why do Christ's sufferings avail as a substitute for man's punishment ? Paul answers by saying, because they are an adequate demonstration of the divine righteousness. The further inquiry, What is there in these sufferings which renders them a vindication of God's holiness and a satisfaction to the law ? is much more difficult to answer by appeal to the apostle's language."[3] We appear to have, then, in what fol-

[1] Bushnell's *Forgiveness and Law*, especially chapter i.
[2] Smyth's *The Orthodoxy of To-day*, p. 174.
[3] Stevens's *The Pauline Theology*, p. 247.

lows, to use an expression which I cannot help
repeating, a re-working of the general teaching
of Paul that Christ by his suffering and death accomplished an atonement, without any reference
to the specific teaching of Paul on the subject.
Professor Stevens, in his development of the
theme, insists on two points. One is the sympathetic identification of Christ with man in his
sinful condition. The other is his testimony by
suffering with and for man to sin's desert of punishment. " God," he tells us, " is rendered favorable to man's forgiveness by the work of Christ
in the sense that an adequate revelation of his
righteousness against sin is made in his sufferings." [1] The first of these points is similar to the
view of Campbell and Dorner. The second is, so
far as I have noticed, peculiar to Dr. Stevens.
While I cannot regard it as expressing the
thought of Paul, as, indeed, it does not profess
to do, it seems to me to be the least artificial
and therefore the best among the suggestions
that I have thus grouped together. The willingness of Christ to suffer and die in the battle
against sin is a testimony to his sense of the
evil of sin, and may easily be taken as repre-

[1] Stevens's *The Pauline Theology*, p. 250.

senting or involving the divine condemnation of it. The artificiality in the position appears when this is made the formal basis of a possible forgiveness of sin by God.

While Professor Stevens makes little attempt to find a special Pauline authority for his interpretation, Professor Du Bose continually refers to the language of Paul.[1] His object appears to be, however, not to reach Paul's thought by a study of his words, but to show that Paul's words are not opposed to the view of the atonement which he urges. His attempt is ingenious. Without quoting literally, I am sure that I express his thought when I say that it affirms that whatever Paul asserts to be true *formally* is so because it is true *actually*. If the term "justification," for instance, has a forensic meaning, this forensic meaning assumes a substantial meaning. If God in a legal sense justifies the sinner, it is because He has already made him just, or has set in motion the agency that should eventually make him just. We have thus the Socinian doctrine united with a recognition of a certain forensic use of language by Paul. The point of de-

[1] Du Bose, *Soteriology of the New Testament.* Cf. pp. 47 ff. and 90 ff.

parture is the traditional view of the atonement. Since this opposes the moral sense of Professor Du Bose, the offending elements must be left out of it. On the other hand, it is assumed that Paul's statements must also be in accord with our moral sense. Thus we have an attempt at a general reconciliation. Paul's expressions are explained in a roundabout manner. A result is reached to which they may be made to conform after a fashion, but which they would not have suggested. There is no index to Professor Du Bose's work, and I would not trust too confidently to my memory; but I do not recall, nor do I find in the portions of his work where it would naturally be expected, any reference to such important texts as, " I, through the law, died unto the law," [1] and " Christ redeemed us from the curse of the law, having become a curse for us : for it is written, ' Cursed is every one that hangeth on a tree.' " [2] I notice, also, that in the carefully indexed work of Professor Stevens there is no reference to the first of these passages. I do not doubt that these acute and learned theologians could explain these verses in harmony with their views ; though, perhaps, the explana-

---

[1] Galatians ii. 19.   [2] Galatians iii. 13.

tion would be a forced one. If they are not referred to, it can be only because these passages
are not vital and essential, so far as their theory
is concerned. With Paul, however, they were
vital and essential. They are not passages to be
explained in accordance with any preconceived
theory. They are passages from which, if we
are to reach any true notion of what Paul actually taught, we should make our start.

Professor Beyschlag, in his " Neutestamentliche Theologie," takes a view which is substantially the same as that maintained by Professor
Du Bose. In defending it he courageously at-
tacks passages which Professor Du Bose, perhaps
more prudently, left unnoticed. If anything
were needed to show the unscriptural character
of the theory, it might be found in Professor
Beyschlag's interpretation, if such it may be
called, of one of the passages just referred to,
namely, Galatians iii. 13. In explaining this passage, he says : " In the crucifixion, Christ gave
himself up to the uttermost that man could in-
flict upon him, and is, thereby, the trustworthy
pledge of God's willingness to forgive. . . . Christ
could by his death free men from the curse of
the law only so far as he freed them from the

whole legal relation to God ; that is, so far as he changed the external, threatening, cursing law into an impelling law of spirit and life, working from within. We here come back to the effect of Christ's death upon the soul of the believer, as constituting its only power." [1]

Conclusion.

I do not refer to these views in order to defend or to criticise them. They are at once ingenious and interesting. So far as all except the two last mentioned are concerned, they make, however, as was said before, no claim that they represent the teaching of the New Testament. So far as they are concerned, Paul might simply have written that Christ was set forth as a propitiation for our sins. All his more definite statements are left wholly out of the account. We have merely a re-working of the general theme. What is important for us here is the fact that these modern efforts illustrate the development of the doctrine of the atonement throughout the history of the church. It has been a theoretical process. The various theologians, if they have referred to the New Testa-

[1] Beyschlag, *Neutestamentliche Theologie*, ii. 156.

ment at all, have contented themselves for the most part with reference to one or two expressions of Paul that illustrated their view. Some, like Anselm, have not done even this.

I do not here dispute the authority of the church and the possibility of a development of doctrine that shall be in its results as important as the statements of Paul himself. It is not my purpose in this discussion to ask what is in itself true, but simply to ask what Paul actually taught. My object is not dogmatic, but exegetical and historical. When we have discovered what was definitely the thought of Paul, we may give to it what worth we will.

My attempt thus far has been to show that the current theory of the manner in which men are justified by the death of Christ derives no support from the significance which had been attached to sacrificial rites either by Gentile or Jew, and further, that this theory derives no support from the history of its genesis and development. Indeed, in view of both the nature of sacrifice in general and the history of the development of Christian doctrine, the presumption would be suggested that the current doctrine is false rather than that it is true. We have found

that the sacrificial idea involved, certainly very
rarely, I believe not at all, the notion of penal
substitution. If we turn to the history of doctrine, we find that, through the greater period
of the history of the church, a view of the efficiency of Christ's death prevailed diametrically
opposite to that which has more recently been
current, namely, that it was a price paid to
the devil. The germ of the doctrine that succeeded this first received historic importance
in the writings of Anselm, who based his view
upon theoretical considerations and not upon the
language of the New Testament. We might say
that this doctrine rested at first solely upon the
"*convenit*" and "*non convenit*" of this somewhat
erratic thinker. The development of the doctrine has been for the most part similar in nature. It was an internal development rather
than an attempt to discover what Paul actually
taught. The idea had been taken from him that
in some way the death of Christ served for the
justification of man, and this theme was wrought
out in the manner that seemed to the theologians from time to time most reasonable. When
any form of the doctrine was suggested or defended by reference to the New Testament, this

procedure was of a haphazard rather than of a
scientific nature. Some striking phrase used by
Paul would be seized upon, and the thought that
it happened to suggest maintained with very little regard to his general teaching. Indeed, any
other method was hardly possible. Exegesis
had not become a science. Interpretation of
the Bible was capricious and often fantastic. It
is only in comparatively recent years that the
study of the New Testament has been in any
degree scientific. I conceive, then, that the fact
that the doctrine which teaches that Christ in
some form or other suffered the penalty due to
man, or paid the debt due from him, has held
possession of the church for some centuries, furnishes no presumption as to the Pauline character of this dogma. On the contrary, I conceive
that the manner in which this general view arose
and has developed itself furnishes a presumption
against its Pauline character. If a theory of the
atonement wrought out of his own head by such
a peculiar, we might say such a queer, thinker
as Anselm could contain in any sense the doctrine which Paul actually taught, it would seem
that such conformity could be only the result of
a wonderful chance or a stupendous miracle.

Yet it is this conceit of Anselm that has been the germ of the successive views which since his day have claimed, with right, the authority of the church, and which are still largely current.

We may, indeed, assume that at this point or any other a miracle has been wrought; that is, we may assume that the doctrinal development of the church has been under divine guidance. It is obvious, however, that such a view could be urged in regard to no particular time and to no particular doctrine. The doctrine that under varying forms, since the time of Anselm, has been specially defended by the church has held this favored position for less than a half of our Christian history, and is already showing signs of having passed the maximum point of its acceptance. It is losing its power, and there is no tendency, so far as I can see, to the general adoption of any other doctrine that shall take its place. If it still held its place, however, as it has done in former years, the doctrine of an inspired church could not be used in its favor. Such a claim could have been made in the ninth century in favor of the diabolical theory as well as in the nineteenth century in favor of the penal-substitutionary theory. If the present age were the last in the history of the church and of the world, there might be more reason for assuming that the church had been guided into the truth. There is, however, no reason to suppose that we are nearing the end. We must drop from our thought of the present period of doctrinal development the importance which is the result of our own relation to it. The time will come when the last two centuries and the last eight centuries will take their place by the side of the centuries that preceded them, — the eighteenth and the nineteenth being no more worthy to claim authority than the eighth and the ninth. This being so, the fact that a certain theory in regard to the atonement has, with certain modifications, been accepted by the church during the past few centuries gives it no stronger claim to be considered as representing Paul's view than could have been made for the doctrine prevalent in the eighth and ninth centuries.

CHAPTER III.

THE TRADITIONAL VIEW UNSCRIPTURAL.

Preliminary Considerations.

ALTHOUGH the theologians who have in successive ages wrought out the system of the atonement which is most widely accepted to-day did this with little attention to the language of the New Testament, what shall we say when we find the result of this development of doctrine accepted, with more or less modification, by the critical students of the New Testament in our own day ? The modern students of the New Testament manifest a learning and a fairness which cannot be too highly praised. Does not the fact that they, to so large an extent, give to the traditional view their indorsement lend to it fresh authority ? Does it not imply that either the marvellous coincidence or the stupendous miracle of which I spoke has been accomplished ? All that can be said is that these students have accepted the results which had been reached by an uncritical age. No other explanation of the Pauline phraseology suggested itself; they therefore undertook to interpret the New Testament as nearly as possible in accordance with the received doctrine of the church. This they have done in good faith and with much ingenuity. So far as their results are concerned, they rest upon nothing which does not admit of a test. Their basis is clearly set forth, and we can determine for ourselves what confidence we may place in it. In point of fact, the result is heterogeneous. There is some forcing of the doctrine, and some forcing of the language of the New Testament. The outcome is inharmonious and self-contradictory. The traditional theory seems at a superficial glance to conform to the phraseology of Paul. A careful examination shows that the resemblance is only superficial, even so far as the texts most relied upon are concerned. This doctrine is like a ready-made garment, which may possess a general conformity to the bodily structure of the person who bought it, but of which the most skilful tailor cannot make a perfect fit. These statements I shall now proceed to defend by such examination of the language of Paul as may seem necessary for this purpose.

I must first express the great indebtedness of the world to the careful scholarship that has been given to the New Testament. Though it has not, as I conceive, reached the true interpretation of Paul's teaching, it has made it possible to reach this. It has settled to a very large extent the meaning of words and the significance of grammatical forms. What Paul said can, with the certainty of a fair amount of accuracy, be said after him in English. Further, the study of experts has given us an accurate idea of at least some aspects of the spiritual and intellectual environment in the midst of which Christianity had its rise. Such a work, for instance, as Weber's "System der Palästinischen Theologie" is invaluable to those for whom are closed the original sources from which such information is derived. By all these results the element of caprice is confined within comparatively small limits. For myself, I will say that in what follows I have not in a single instance attempted to force, or escape from, the limitations which the best students of the New Testament have established. I have accepted from the hands of experts the most exact results which they could offer. Happily I have been under no temptation to do otherwise. The more strictly the letter of the Pauline epistles has been accepted, the more clearly did the statements they contain lend themselves to the interpretation which I was striving to present. I think that Paul's teaching has been misunderstood, because his words have not been taken literally enough. Some preconceived notion of what tradition has made him say, or of what the commentator thinks that he ought to have said, comes between the critic and his text, and the strict significance of his words has often been lost sight of.

I have affirmed that in most cases we can repeat Paul's teaching in English, with the confidence that we represent it fairly well. What he meant by what he said is another question. The critical students of the New Testament have made the interpretation of Paul's teaching possible. In some most important matters I believe that they have not interpreted it aright. They are, as I conceive, like expert woodsmen who are trying to force their way through a difficult region. They have started in at the point which tradition indicated, and have fought their way manfully and skilfully. They have hewn a path through jungles ; they have somehow bridged chasms, and have climbed over, or wound about, opposing cliffs. All that I claim is, that in my wanderings I have happened upon a trail by which advance is so pleasant and easy that I cannot help believing it to be the original one that was blazed by Paul himself. Without a tithe of the woodcraft which these heroic workers possess, I yet venture to ask them just to try this new path, and see if it is not vastly easier than the one along which they have been struggling.

In the present chapter I shall point out two or three of the difficulties to which I have just referred. I shall try to show that the traditional interpretation runs against obstacles at every turn. In the next chapter I shall show how the interpretation that I suggest adapts itself at every point to the most literal treatment of the language of the apostle and of his school.

Two Assumptions.

Before entering upon this examination, it is important to recognize two principles which may be taken for granted at the outset. One of these is the assumption that the thought of Paul, so far as we are here concerned with it, was definite and permanent. He referred, indeed, to the death of Christ in many ways and in many different relations. Sometimes his reference to it was literal, often it was symbolical. Thus the death of Christ constantly assumed in his thought a fresh significance, and manifested itself under varying aspects. So far, however, as Paul used forensic language in regard to the death of Christ, so far, that is, as he had to do with the abolition of the law and the remission of sins, we must assume that his thought was definite and practically unchanging. So far as this aspect of the death of Christ is concerned, we must assume that, in the words of Paul, we have to do with no mere figure of speech, but with what he regarded as a definite fact, and with results that he believed actually to flow from it. Nothing less fixed or definite than this would have sufficed for the accomplishment of such a mighty revolution as that which was produced by the preaching of Paul. We assume, then, that all the language used by Paul in regard to the great matters under consideration meant substantially the same thing.

In what I have just said, I have spoken of the abolition of the law and of the remission of sins,

as though they were parts of the same transaction. Paul presents two aspects of the death of
Christ : the forensic and the moral. The forensic includes the two elements just named, the
abolition of the law and the remission of sins.
It could hardly be expected that the death of
Christ should have had two forensic results,
which were independent of one another. My
assumption is, then, that in Paul's thought the
one forensic effect of the death of Christ included both the results, as different aspects of
the same thing. Perhaps, however, I should
rather call this a presumption, leaving the
stronger word " assumption " to refer to the fact
that in the thought of Paul the forensic aspect
of the case was always the same.

The second principle that we must assume is,
that in trying to reach this fixed and definite
thought of Paul, the expressions that are more
abstract are to be explained by those that are
more concrete. A little thought will make the
truth and the importance of this assumption
obvious. The more abstract statements admit
of various significations. When it is said, for
instance, in general, that we are saved or justified through the death or through the blood of

Christ, there is no hint as to the precise manner in which this result is accomplished. Such passages admit of various explanations. On the other hand, the more concrete a passage is, the fewer explanations are possible. One that is absolutely and definitely concrete would admit of only one explanation. Such a passage, if indeed such an one may be found to exist, should be used to give a definite significance to the statements that are more abstract.

I imagine that, as thus stated, both of these assumptions will be granted. In fact, however, the second has not been practically recognized. The theologians, even the commentators, have to a very large extent based their results upon the more general and abstract statements of Paul. The more concrete statements have been too often touched lightly upon, as something accidental, or at least as something not essential. Even Professor Pfleiderer, who holds more closely than most to the specific language of Paul, expresses with great frankness the slight estimation in which Paul's definite argumentation is held by him. Professor Pfleiderer says of Paul, that " he proves his thesis through exegetical deductions, which are rather far-fetched and not always quite conclusive, in regard to which it is very obvious that they are used simply to give an outward support to what the apostle held upon quite other and inner grounds." [1] I think it may be said with truth that the theologians have too often fancied that they understood the matter better than Paul himself. My simple assumption is that Paul knew what he was talking about, and that he meant precisely what he said ; and that if we want to understand him, the one thing for us to do is to follow his own reasoning as closely and as literally as we can. If any reader doubts whether this method will lead to any good result, I beg that he will at least be willing to make the experiment.

The " Curse " of Christ.

The passage which is the most definite and concrete of any in the epistles of Paul in regard to the matter that we are considering is the famous thirteenth verse of the third chapter of the Epistle to the Galatians. " Christ redeemed us from the curse of the law, having become a curse for us, for it is written, Cursed is every one that hangeth on a tree." I have said that this pas-

[1] *Paulinismus*, second edition, p. 6.

sage is the most definite in the writings of Paul
in regard to the atonement that Paul believed
to have been accomplished through the death of
Christ.   This is true in regard to its statement
of the curse which Christ underwent, through
which the Christian was redeemed from the law.
In what manner his endurance of the curse
worked for man's redemption it does not tell us.
This we shall have to seek elsewhere.

The curse which Christ underwent was that
pronounced against all " who hang upon a tree."
In the Jewish law, as among all earlier peoples,
many things were associated together which we
are in the habit of distinguishing. Different kinds
of commandment and of offences, of purity and
of impurity, were all placed upon the same level.
These commands and these different forms of
impurity we may divide into those that were
strictly religious, those that were ethical, and
those that were ceremonial.   We have examples
of all these in the ten commandments.   " Thou
shalt love the Lord thy God" is purely religious.
The command, " Thou shalt not kill," is ethical.
The command, " Thou shalt remember the Sabbath day to keep it holy," is ceremonial.   The
Hebrews, we may suppose, made no distinction

between these different kinds of commandment. They all rested upon the same authority. Even to the Puritan in England and in America there was no difference between these commandments. To break the Sabbath was as truly a crime as theft or murder.

I have used the word "ceremonial" for lack of a better, and in a sense negative rather than positive. I have meant to say that there were laws which were without religious or ethical significance. There were, corresponding to these, forms of purity and impurity which were also without religious or moral signification. Some of these may have had originally a hygienic value; but for the most it would be impossible to give any explanation which would not be conjectural and arbitrary. Such forms of purity and impurity had no relation to the purpose which accompanied the polluting act, or even to the consciousness of those who were concerned. The regulations under which such varied forms of pollution become possible may be summed up under what it has become common to designate as the law of "Taboo." The word is a helpful one, though it stands for a confused mass of things differing widely among themselves, about which we know accurately little or nothing.

Of this sort was the curse that is referred to in the statement of Paul which I have just quoted. It is generally understood that the passage from the book of Deuteronomy that Paul quotes referred to the habit of hanging certain criminals, in some way or other, after they had been otherwise killed.[1] However this may be, the persons thus suspended were in the eye of the law impure, and if they remained in this position over night, the land would suffer from the presence of these impure objects. They were " cursed before God." That this view of the impurity attached to crucifixion continued may be seen in the passage of the fourth Gospel which tells how the execution of Jesus and the thieves was hurried, because the next Sabbath was a high day.[2]

We can now understand the nature of the curse that Christ underwent. It arose from the form of his death. It was because he was crucified that he was accursed. We here reach the centre of Paul's thought and the essential thing in his argument. It is a thing that has been too often overlooked ; but so far as we

[1] Deuteronomy xxi. 22, 23.
[2] John's Gospel, xix. 31.

overlook it, we fail utterly to understand what
Paul is talking about. It is important to notice
that Christ was accursed because he was crucified. He was not crucified because he was accursed.

We see now that very important results may
follow from the second assumption that was
made above; — the assumption, namely, that the
more concrete statements made by Paul must
be used to explain the more abstract. Whenever the death of Christ or the blood of Christ
is referred to as the means by which the Christian is justified, or by which atonement has been
made, such references are to be explained by the
passage we have just considered. In this way
and in no other did Christ, in the thought of
Paul, undergo for man the curse of the law. The
manner of his death made him ceremonially impure.

We shall later ask what are the positive conclusions to be drawn from this fact. At present
we have to use it negatively, and to notice how
the current theory of the atonement is affected
by it.

The traditional theory, being based upon the
more abstract statements of Paul, is itself, in the

form in which it is generally held, abstract, and thus admits of various interpretations. The central article of belief is that Christ bore the penalty which men had deserved. What was precisely the nature of the penalty that he bore is explained in various ways. Thus Professor Shedd held that "the essence of the atonement is in the suffering"[1] of Christ. In this suffering was included not only the pain connected with his death, but that of his entire life. Dr. Alfred Cave, on the other hand, insists that the death of Christ was the essential thing.[2] In this he goes back to the thought of Anselm. Christ, being sinless, needed not to die, and by dying he thus underwent that which could not have been demanded of him. Dr. Cave adds to this the fact that to Paul death was the penalty of human transgression. Christ, being without sin, in dying suffered what he had not deserved, and bore for those who should believe in him the penalty of their sins. Dr. Cave claims that his view is based upon induction, that is, upon a careful and comparative study of the utterances of the New Testament. He, however, seems to have over-

[1] *Dogmatic Theology*, p. 414, *et passim*.
[2] *Scriptural Doctrine of Sacrifice*, pp. 312 ff.

looked the passages that throw most light upon the matter ; or at least to have given them only superficial attention.

The passage in Paul's Epistle to the Galatians which we have been considering is fatal to both these theories. So far as Professor Shedd's notion is concerned, that the suffering was the essential thing, it is obvious that this could have had no place in the thought of Paul. The curse that Christ bore resulted from the form of his death. In regard to the original statement in the book of Deuteronomy, the explanation generally given is, as we have seen, that the bodies of those already slain were hanged upon the tree, and thus became impure and a source of impurity. The suffering had been already passed when the act that was analogous to crucifixion took place. Neither could the death of Christ be, as Dr. Cave insists, the element in which the essence of the act consisted. If the theory of Dr. Cave were correct, it would not have mattered what manner of death Christ underwent. He might have died in his bed, or by any accident, or by any other form of execution, and the result would have been the same. In Paul's thought he bore the curse for his followers by being *cru-*

cified. When Paul speaks of Christ as the crucified, he means precisely this. It was this form
of death which the law pronounced accursed, and
we have no right to put death in general in the
place of this, and imagine that Paul's reasoning
would still hold.

So far as the more general statements of the
current doctrine are concerned, they are so very
vague and involve so closely other aspects of the
case, that the passage that we have been considering cannot, taken by itself, be satisfactorily
used as the test of their truth. I am inclined to
think, however, that in many cases in which the
traditional doctrine is expressed in a general way,
either the view held by Dr. Shedd or that held by
Dr. Cave is really assumed, or that both the suffering and the death of Christ are assumed as the
necessary basis of the transaction. Sometimes
the idea of a curse of which the crucifixion is in
some sense the expression is thought of. Of this
we shall see examples later. I have seen no statement of the doctrine which recognized the simple
and clear utterance of Paul, namely, that Christ
became accursed solely by the fact that he was
crucified.

The Abolition of the Law.

As, however, it is difficult to apply to merely general statements the test of this passage in such a way as to demonstrate their unpauline character, we shall be forced to take in connection with it a passage from the same epistle, which describes another aspect of the death of Christ. The statement which we have now to introduce is found in the nineteenth and twentieth verses of the second chapter of the Epistle to the Galatians : " For I through the law died unto the law, that I might live unto God. I have been crucified with Christ."

This passage, like the one before quoted, has been made prominent in the theories and the discussions of theologians ; but like that it has been often treated in a vague and general way, with little regard to its special significance. It is the complement of the other passage, indicating the manner in which the fact that Christ bore the curse works for the redemption of the Christian from the curse of the law ; as the other stated the nature of the curse which Christ bore.

We will first apply this verse to the current doctrine as it is generally held, and will then consider the manner in which it and the passage previously considered have been explained by those who have given them special attention.

The doctrine as generally held assumes that Christ in his death bore the penalty for men's sins, and that therefore those who believe in him are free from the penalty that they deserved, and are also free from any obligation to obey the Jewish law. Let us see how this agrees with the statement of Paul just quoted.

This statement of Paul involves two elements. One is that the Christian is free from the law; the other is that this freedom from the law is reached through the law itself. He says, "I through the law died unto the law." We will, for convenience, consider first the second of these principles, namely, that the abrogation of the law comes through the law itself.

The theologians claim that the Christian is free from the law, because Christ has suffered the punishment which the sins of his followers had deserved. As it is more commonly put, the sacrifices appointed by the law were the types of which the death of Christ was the antitype. When the antitype was accomplished, the types and all the observances of the law became obsolete. This result is obviously, however, nothing that has been reached through the law itself. It is not a fulfilment of the law, but an abrogation of it. The sacrifices, for instance, may have pointed to the great sacrifice on Calvary ; but there was in them nothing to lead to the accomplishment of this. The law held its place till a mightier than it came, and then it gave way before him. In all this there is nothing to explain the cry of Paul, " I *through the law* died unto the law."

It has been said, indeed, that through the educational effect of the law those placed under it had reached a point where they no longer needed it, and thus died to the law through the law ; as, since death is the natural end of life, we may be said through life to die to life. Since "the law," it has been urged, "hath been our tutor to bring us unto Christ," [1] when it has brought us to Christ its function is accomplished. Itself leads us out of itself. There could be no better example than this of the vague way in which Paul's clear and direct utterances are often interpreted. In point of fact, men had not through the law become so trained that they could go on

[1] Galatians iii. 24.

without it. It was not like a school which dismisses its scholars when they have become perfect. The law had, according to Paul,[1] shown its absolute inadequacy to produce this result. What, then, did Paul mean when he said that the law had been the tutor to bring men to Christ? We may try to answer this question later. All that concerns us now is that it could not have been by educating men up to the point where it was needless. The law failed to make men righteous. It was suddenly superseded. "What the law could not do, in that it was weak through the flesh, God, sending his own Son in the likeness of sinful flesh and as an offering for sin, condemned sin in the flesh."[2] Paul says that this annulling of the law was accomplished by the law itself. I maintain that the current interpretations of his teaching give no hint as to how this paradoxical statement can be true. Till this statement, which Bengel called *summa ac medulla Christianismi*,[3] presents a clear and definite meaning, one fitted to hold good in a court of law, we have no idea of Paul's doctrine.

It is further difficult to see how, according to

[1] Romans viii. 36, *et passim*.   [2] Romans viii. 3.
[3] See Meyer, a. l.

the current theory of Paul's teaching, the Christian could, in any way, have become free of the law. Granted all that the theory claims, that Christ actually suffered the penalty of the world's sin, what is there in this that should lead to the abrogation of the divinely appointed law? Because at the cost of the blood of Christ men were relieved from the penalty that they most justly had deserved, is that any reason why they should disregard the law against which they had sinned? Was the law to be obeyed simply to escape its penalty; and because provision has been made against this, does the law itself become of no account? We might understand why the typical sacrifices should be no longer needed when the antitype had come; but why should other portions of the law, — that of the Sabbath and of circumcision, for instance, — things that had no relation to the atonement, why should these also be given up?

In a word, the law was to Paul a divinely appointed thing. Only the power that ordained it could repeal it. Only the law itself could put an end to itself. When Paul said, "I through the law died unto the law," he described the only process by which for him the law could be annulled. The current view fails to show how the law put an end to itself, and thus how it was actually done away with.

The Interpretation of Pfleiderer and Weizsäcker.

We have thus considered in relation to the two passages which have been quoted from the Epistle to the Galatians the current view as it is presented by theologians in general. These can elaborate their doctrines with greater or less attention to the language of the New Testament, as they may find it convenient or interesting. The case is different with the theologians who make a special study of the New Testament. They can overlook nothing. We have now to see how such writers reconcile the current theological views with the passages from Paul which we have been considering.

Midway between the theologians, as such, and the commentators stands Professor Pfleiderer, whose " Paulinismus " is one of the most interesting and suggestive works upon this theme.

Professor Pfleiderer urges that in the view of Paul the law was no longer binding, because it was no longer necessary. He says : " If the crucifixion of Christ is recognized as the divinely appointed means by which righteousness is to be obtained, then it follows that the law is no longer the means. The crucifixion of Christ is thus the end of the law." [1] Further, Professor Pfleiderer tells us, the law is not only needless by the side of the means of salvation offered by Christ; the two methods are wholly incompatible. He says : "That could not be a righteousness according to the law which was brought by one who by the law was accursed. That must be a wholly new righteousness, a righteousness without any relation to the law. . . . Under such a Messiah the whole religious world of the Jews must pass away and give place to a new." [2]

Professor Weizsäcker also assumes that in the presence of the righteousness that is by faith, the law would disappear of itself. He says : "As through the death of Jesus the sin in the flesh is destroyed, so is the law destroyed." [3] And again : "As through Christ man has died to sin, he has died to the law also; he is free from it."

The view of these eminent writers that the

[1] Pfleiderer's *Der Paulinismus* (second edition), pp. 6 f.

[2] *Ibid.* p. 11.

[3] Weizsäcker's *Das Apostolische Zeitalter der Christlichen Kirche*, p. 136.

law ceased simply because another way of salvation was recognized seems to me to meet neither the probabilities of the case nor the teaching of Paul. In the first place, it does not meet the probabilities of the case. I can conceive that the law, being superseded, should gradually become less and less recognized, and that it should thus fade out by slow degrees. I cannot conceive that the presence of another way of salvation should lead to that sudden and absolute dismission of the entire law which we find to have been accomplished in the case of Paul. In the second place, it is certain that such a view has nothing in common with the sharp, ringing cry of Paul: " I *through the law* died unto the law." [1] With Paul's view of the divine authority of the law, there was no place for reasoning whether it was of any further use or not. It was not for him to question or decide. It was for him simply to obey until release should come through the law itself. This cry of Paul must have referred to no general incompatibility, but to something as definite as the cry itself. Notice the force of the aorist in this passage: " I died to the law." This refers to a moment, to

[1] Galatians ii. 19.

an act. It implies that, so far as the Christian is concerned, the death on the cross, by its essential nature, suddenly abolished the law.

As to the method by which the death of Christ took the place of the punishment which the sinner had deserved, Pfleiderer's statements lack the clearness which marks the greater part of his discussion. He says of the words which describe Christ as having been made a curse for us, that they "do not say that Christ became personally an accursed one or the object of the divine wrath, since, on the contrary, he as the sinless Son of God has been the object of the unchanging love of God ; but they say only that Christ allowed to be fulfilled upon himself the curse of the punishment of death to which the sinful world was doomed. Since he died the death on the cross, which by the law itself is expressly branded as the death of malefactors, he has given to the law the required atonement which it demanded for sin ; and because the sin was not his but ours, he accomplished the atonement in our stead, and thereby redeemed us from the threatened curse of the law which otherwise would have rested upon us." [1]

[1] Pfleiderer's *Paulinismus* (second edition), pp. 135 f.

This passage seems to me to present a confusion of ideas rather than anything that the mind can grasp distinctly. So far as the first part of the passage is concerned, it is true that Paul does not say that Christ was the object of the divine wrath. He does say, however, that Christ was himself accursed; for no expression could state this more strongly than that which says that he " became a curse." As the passage that I have quoted from Professor Pfleiderer goes on, it is not clear in what way Christ is supposed to have borne the penalty of human sin. In one line we are told that he took the punishment of death upon himself, which seems to imply a view similar to that of Dr. Cave and of Anselm, namely, that death is the punishment of sin, and that Christ in dying suffered that which he had not deserved. In the next line the fact that this death was a shameful one, being that on the cross, is specified as the means by which the penalty of the law was fulfilled. These two ideas are not only distinct from one another; they are incompatible. If death was the penalty which man deserved, but which Christ bore without deserving it, we have something complete in itself. It does not matter by what death he died.

Whatever shame or curse was specially attached to the cross can add nothing to the significance of the transaction. If, on the other hand, the special obloquy attached to the cross had anything to do with the transaction, it must have had everything to do with it. In this case, Christ did not suffer what was due to man. It was a suffering peculiar to himself which, in some way, took the place of what man had deserved. Further, the law does not say that death by the cross is a malefactor's death. It says that he that hangs upon a tree is accursed. Further, it is not true that Christ had not exposed himself to this curse. He had exposed himself to it without his will, it is true, in the fact that he was crucified. I repeat what I said in substance before. The law does not say the accursed are crucified, but that the crucified are accursed. Christ in being crucified became, on his own account, the object of the curse. Primarily he did not suffer a curse that belonged to men; he suffered one which was due to himself, because he found himself in the position against which the curse of the law is uttered.

Meyer's Interpretation.

In his " Paulinismus," Professor Pfleiderer de-
velops, with more or less freedom, what he conceived to be the ideas of Paul. He has, of course,
to refer to the language of Paul. He is not
forced, however, to follow this, step by step.
This complete and minute examination is what
the commentator of the New Testament is obliged
to make ; and we might expect that this necessity of a minute examination of Paul's utterances,
on the one side, and the supposed necessity of
harmonizing them with the traditional, theological notions, on the other, would accomplish a
result still more confused and unintelligible. I
do not mean that this necessity is anything external, laid upon the commentator from without,
but that, assuming the traditional view to be the
true one, he feels obliged to explain, if possible,
the statements of Paul in accordance with this.

As we took the work of Pfleiderer as being
the most recent and the best special work on the
subject, so we will take " Meyer's Commentary "
as being the best and most widely recognized
work of its class.

I dislike to make what might seem flippant

criticism on works to which I am so much indebted; but the matter appears to me so demonstrably clear and certain that I must simply present it in the only way that is possible to me.

In his discussion of the matter, Meyer introduces two wholly different conceptions without apparently perceiving their irreconcilable character. He speaks of Christ as actually becoming by his crucifixion the object of the divine ὀργή.[1] Why Meyer uses the word ὀργή instead of "wrath" is not clear; for it is a word that is never used in the New Testament to express the relation between Christ and the Father. On the contrary, in the Epistle to the Ephesians, we read that Christ "gave himself up for us, an offering and a sacrifice to God for an odor of a sweet smell."[2] This expression refers to the crucifixion, and would appear to exclude the idea of wrath, whether expressed in Greek or English. In Meyer's Commentary, this passage is referred to in a note, with an unsatisfactory suggestion of the manner in which it may be reconciled with the idea that he was at the moment an object of wrath. That Christ could stand at the same moment as an object of the divine wrath and as a

[1] Meyer on Galatians iii. 13. [2] Ephesians v. 2.

sacrifice of sweet odor is impossible. It will be remembered that Professor Pfleiderer discards the notion of wrath, although he still holds Christ to have borne the penalty of the world's sin. In connection with this notion of the divine anger, Meyer introduces the conception of an offence against the law which demands a certain penalty, and is satisfied when this penalty has been fulfilled. " Because, now that the law has accomplished in his case its rights, the bond of union which joined him to the law is broken." In the Christian, who is said to be " crucified with Christ," "the curse of the law is likewise fulfilled, so that in virtue of his ethical fellow-ship in the death of Jesus, he knows himself to be dead διά νόμου, and consequently at the same time dead *to the law*." [1]

What is meant in this passage by the words "ethical fellowship," through which the Chris-tian is crucified with Christ and shares the bene-fit of his suffering the curse of the law, is, I con-fess, to me wholly incomprehensible. Another thing that is incomprehensible is the relation between the divine anger, on the one side, and the law which is silenced when its penalty is

[1] Meyer on Galatians ii. 19.

inflicted, on the other. The former is something
real and spiritual ; the latter is something technical and formal. Can we suppose that Paul
taught that the righteous indignation of God
could satisfy itself by a single flash ? If so, it
would appear as if the outcasts in hell should be
made free after the first shock.

Hebrews ix. 13, 14.

If we now leave these two passages which are
central in the whole discussion, and glance at
those which are more general in their form, we
notice something which is very strange, if the
traditional interpretation of the New Testament
teaching is correct. I refer to the fact that the
writers of the New Testament continually stop
short, or turn aside, just when they might be expected to state this doctrine. Instead of multi-
plying quotations, I will take a single passage
from the Epistle to the Hebrews, an epistle which
is recognized as belonging, on the whole, to the
Pauline school. The writer of this epistle says :
" For if the blood of goats and bulls, and the
ashes of a heifer sprinkling them that have been
defiled, sanctify unto the cleanness of the flesh :
how much more shall the blood of Christ, who

through the eternal Spirit offered himself without blemish unto God, *cleanse your conscience from dead works to serve the living God ?* " [1]

The words which I have italicized are certainly not those with which a modern theologian of the traditional school would have closed this passage. Superficially considered, they would seem to favor rather the interpretation of the Socinians than that of the orthodox theologian. Looked at closely, they favor neither.

I have selected this passage because it would have afforded such a fine opportunity for the writer to the Hebrews to introduce the idea which the church has in these later centuries upheld, if only it had been in his mind. The passage is a typical one. In a word, the traditional doctrine has to be read into the more abstract statements of the New Testament, and cannot be reconciled with those that are more concrete and definite.

Conclusion.

Many other passages that illustrate the unscriptural character of the current view of Paul's doctrine of the atonement can be better dis-

[1] Hebrews ix. 13, 16.

cussed in connection with the consideration of their real meaning. In bringing forward two or three passages from the New Testament to illustrate the inadequacy of the traditional interpretation, I have wished simply to prepare the way for a more candid and interested examination of the view that I am about to present than might otherwise have been possible.

CHAPTER IV.

THE GOSPEL OF PAUL.

Sources.

As, after all this preparation, we approach the positive treatment of our theme, we are met by the difficulty that we nowhere have a first-hand and systematic statement by Paul of his doctrine. In every case he is writing to those who are already familiar with the principles upon which his teaching was based. All his utterances are fragmentary. The Epistle to the Galatians throws more light upon his position than any other of his writings; but to the Galatians he had already expounded his doctrine. They were not fresh minds to be taught; they were back-sliders to be reclaimed. From this point of view the epistle is a marvel of effective expostulation; but it is in no sense a systematic treatise. It is interesting to see in how many different moods Paul approaches his old converts, in how many different ways he strives to recall them to their old

faith. He wonders at their inconstancy. " I marvel," he says, " that ye are so quickly removing
. . . unto a different gospel,"[1] which is nothing
that is worthy to be called a gospel. He denounces
the teachers of the strange doctrine : " Though
we, or an angel from heaven, should preach unto
you any gospel other than that which we preached
unto you, let him be anathema."[2] He denounces
those who accept such teaching : " Ye are severed from Christ, ye who would be justified by
the law ; ye are fallen away from grace."[3] He
ridicules them : " O foolish Galatians, who did
bewitch you ? "[4] He praises them : " Ye were
running well ; who did hinder you that ye should
not obey the truth ? "[5] He urges his love for
them : " My little children, of whom I am again
in travail until Christ be formed in you."[6] He
urges their old love for him : " For I bear you
witness, that, if possible, ye would have plucked
out your eyes and given them to me."[7] He uses
argument, indeed, but it is argument so familiar
to them that they need only to be reminded of

[1] Galatians i. 6.   [2] Galatians i. 8.
[3] Galatians v. 4.   [4] Galatians iii. 1.
[5] Galatians v. 7.   [6] Galatians iv. 19.
[7] Galatians iv. 15.

it. He hurls his arguments at them in the form of epigrams : " I through the law died unto the law ; " [1] " Christ redeemed us from the curse of the law, having become a curse for us." [2] These epigrams are less arguments than fragments of arguments. We have to piece them together, and help them out by what Paul or his followers tell us elsewhere. He glorifies his doctrine by showing its relation to the whole history of the past of their nation. He pictures the glory of the liberty to which he calls them : They are no longer bond-servants, they are sons and heirs.[3] In all his zeal for his doctrine, he could not forget that which is more precious than any theory ; and before he closes he summons them to the life of love and holiness : " Be not deceived ; God is not mocked : for whatsoever a man soweth, that shall he also reap." [4] He cannot leave them, however, without warning them against the teachers who do not themselves keep the law, but wish to glory in their flesh.[5] These are only a few of the forms of appeal by which Paul attempts to win back his converts to their former

[1] Galatians ii. 19. [2] Galatians iii. 13.
[3] Galatians iii. 26–29. [4] Galatians vi. 7.
[5] Galatians vi. 13.

faith in the gospel that he preached. There is almost everything except a clear, straightforward statement, such as he would make to one who might be hearing his gospel for the first time.

The Epistle to the Romans, which for our purpose stands next in importance to the Epistle to the Galatians, exhibits the same lack. Paul, indeed, had never met the disciples at Rome face to face. They were, however, familiar with his teachings, and, in spite of what some critics have urged, they sympathized with them. Paul, in writing to them, did not need to express himself as he would have done to those to whom his gospel was something wholly new. He did not need to reason with them as with backsliders from the faith. He needed simply to exhibit his gospel in its larger relations.

Though the Epistle to the Romans resembles that to the Galatians in the lack of a systematic presentation of the fundamental principles of his doctrine, it is like it in little else. Indeed, there is nothing that brings Paul nearer to us, and gives us a stronger sense of his personality, than the variation in the style of his epistles, according to his relation to the church to which he writes. With the Corinthians, in spite of their

lapses from virtue against which he protests, he
seems to have been most at his ease. He appears to have had a special affection for them.
In writing to them his genius shows itself without any constraint. Nowhere in his epistles, and
indeed rarely in the writings of the world, do we
find such outbursts of lofty and fervid eloquence
as he addressed to them. His hymn to charity
and his glowing words in regard to the life after
death stand alone in literature.

With the Romans his relations were very different. He was writing, as we have said, to
strangers. They were sympathetic, but they
were strangers none the less. Moreover, he
seems to have felt that he was writing to the
capital of the world. He seems to have felt
something of the awe which the majesty of the
imperial city might naturally inspire. This did
not repress his genius; it stimulated it. It does,
however, seem to have affected the form of his
expression. The familiarities and the special
outbursts of the other epistles are lacking. In
the place of these there is a dignity which none
of the other epistles possesses. The letter to
the Romans has the loftiness, the sweep, and
the unity of an oration. It shows Paul to have

been not merely a man of fervid eloquence, but equally a master of form. Thus, the Epistle to the Romans stands as the completed monument of Paul's genius. It presents his doctrine in the aspect of a philosophy of history. It was, however, as has been said, addressed to those to whom it was no new thing ; and therefore it does not give in simple and detailed form the principles upon which the whole is based.

The Epistles to the Galatians and to the Romans are the only ones which are specially devoted to the presentation of Paul's gospel ; but in some of the others we find here and there statements and expressions which throw much light upon his system, not the less helpful because they are incidental in discourses which bear mostly upon other themes.

In considering the material from which we have to seek the doctrine of Paul in regard to the atonement, we do not need to trouble ourselves with questions of criticism, and to consider the objections that have been raised against the authenticity of this epistle and that. The doctrine of Paul was substantially the doctrine of a school. It was an important movement which Paul inaugurated. The principles which he defi-

nitely taught formed the basis of the Christian
life of the larger church of which he was the
founder. We should expect that they would be
substantially the same, whether taught by his
followers or himself.

Of course, if in a doubtful epistle there were
any indication of a different view from that which
is presented in those of which the genuineness
is undoubted, the case would be different ; but
so long as the expressions used in a doubtful
epistle are such as adapt themselves perfectly
to the interpretation of Paul's teaching that I
am urging, there is no reason why they should
not be used to illustrate and to defend this interpretation. The Epistles to the Ephesians and
that to the Colossians are the only ones among
the disputed epistles of which I shall make such
use.[1] In what I have said, I have not meant
to express an opinion in a matter in regard to
which my opinion would be worth little. I
merely wish to justify the use that I make of
these epistles, whatever view may be taken of
them.

[1] Of these epistles, Dr. Toy says that, whoever their author or
authors may be, their theology is substantially Pauline. *Judaism
and Christianity*, p. 215.

What I have said of these epistles may be applied to the Epistle to the Hebrews. Nobody now supposes that this epistle was written by Paul. Nobody doubts, so far as I know, that it was written by a follower of Paul. There may be found in it differences from the Pauline teaching. I shall suggest one such possible difference. The movement represented by Paul and the writer to the Hebrews was, however, an extremely definite one, and all its representatives may be assumed to have been inspired by the same thought in regard to the fundamental relation of Christianity to Judaism. I shall, therefore, not hesitate to refer to the Epistle to the Hebrews, and to take what help it may furnish in the attempt to reach a comprehension of Paul's teaching. Certainly, nothing not from the hand of Paul himself can be used so confidently for this purpose as the writings of his followers. In other words, if we had undertaken to discuss the doctrine of atonement as held by the non-Judaizing wing of the apostolic church, all the material just referred to would naturally be used. As Paul was the great leader in the anti-Jewish movement, it matters little whether it is spoken of as his movement or by a more general name.

Our material, then, consists in scattered utterances by Paul, and by one or more representatives of his school, according as we reckon the Epistles to the Ephesians and the Colossians as by Paul or his followers. These scattered utterances we have to fit together as perfectly as we may. If we can unite them, as we will hope, so that they will make a perfect whole, we shall have the most satisfactory result. If anything is to be added, this should not be done till the original pieces have been arranged as far as they will go. We are like a boy with the bits of a dissected map before him, not quite sure whether anything is missing or not. His way is to fit together the pieces that he has, and if anything more is finally needed, to cut out a piece precisely the shape of the empty space.

The Abolition of the Law.

If we turn now to the business in hand, we have to start with the passages from the Epistle to the Galatians which were discussed in the last chapter. The key to the whole matter is found in the thirteenth verse of the third chapter: "Christ redeemed us from the curse of the law, having become a curse for us : for it is written,

Cursed is every one that hangeth on a tree." The nature of this curse was considered in the last chapter. We there saw that, in the Hebrew law as well as in the religious rites of all older peoples, elements which we are in the habit of distinguishing from one another are united. With these are mingled elements of which we have no conception. In that chapter we made an extremely loose but sufficiently practical division between purity and impurity which have an ethical significance and those that are purely ceremonial.[1] In this the earlier codes may be compared to the rays of pure unrefracted light. These rays we divide for our own purposes into the color-bringing rays, the heat-bringing rays, and the chemical rays. The division is artificial, though the distinction is real. So in studying the rules of life of any ancient people, it is necessary to separate elements that were united in their thought.

In the case before us, as we have already seen, the curse under which the crucified suffered was of the nature of ceremonial impurity. He that bore it was not crucified because he was accursed ; he was accursed because he was cruci-

[1] See p. 112 f.

fied. Of course, he who thus bore the curse of the law, being already dead, could not himself suffer from it, except so far as the body might be exposed to some indignity. The significance of the impurity, which was the substance of the curse, consisted in the fact that the thing thus impure became a source of pollution. If the land, as is intimated in the original passage in the book of Deuteronomy,[1] should become polluted through the fact that those who were hung upon a tree remained thus exposed during the night, the result would be, apparently, that the dwellers in the land would suffer some calamity therefrom. Some similar trouble was apparently feared if Jesus and his fellow-sufferers remained thus hanging over the Sabbath, which was one of special sanctity. Thus we read, "The Jews therefore, because it was the Preparation, that the bodies should not remain on the cross upon the sabbath (for the day of that sabbath was a high day), asked of Pilate that their legs might be broken, and that they might be taken away."[2]

Such was the curse under which Paul considered the crucified Jesus to rest.

The nineteenth and twentieth verses of the

---

[1] Deuteronomy xxi. 23.   [2] John xix. 31.

second chapter of the Epistle to the Galatians are, obviously, to be taken in close connection with that just considered : " For I through the law died unto the law, that I might live unto God. I have been crucified with Christ." [1] The sense in which Paul affirmed that he had been crucified with Christ is, after what has been said, unmistakable. The point which Paul emphasizes in regard to the crucifixion is the legal and ceremonial impurity which it involved. When Paul says, " I have been crucified with Christ," he can, therefore, mean nothing else than that he shares with him the legal and ceremonial impurity that was involved in his crucifixion. In other words, Paul, owing to his connection with the crucified, was, like him, legally impure, and was thus an outcast from the Jewish church.

The necessity of this result from Paul's point of view is obvious. As we have seen, the nature of the impurity which marked the body of the crucified was that it became itself a source of pollution. The Christian stood in the closest possible relation with his crucified Lord. His whole spiritual life was derived from him. He made of the crucified his Messiah. Thus, from

[1] Galatians ii. 19, 20.

the Jewish point of view, he brought the accursed thing into the very sanctuary, and gave it there the central and supreme place. No violation of the legal and ceremonial order could be greater, and to the Jew more shocking, than this. The Christian and his Lord were thus together impure and outcasts from the sacred commonwealth of the Jews.

The bearing of all this upon the relation of the Christianized Jew to the law is sufficiently obvious. Instead, however, of letting our own thought press forward to the result which is already in sight, we will let the relation be stated by the writer to the Hebrews, who belonged to the school of Paul, and who, as I have already urged, may be trusted in so fundamental a matter to represent Paul. This writer says : "*We have an altar, whereof they have no right to eat which serve the tabernacle.* For the bodies of those beasts, whose blood is brought into the holy place by the high priest as an offering for sin, are burned without the camp. Wherefore Jesus also, that he might sanctify the people through his own blood, suffered without the gate. Let us, therefore, go forth unto him without the camp, bearing his reproach." [1]

[1] Hebrews xiii. 10–13.

This extremely interesting passage suggests certain aspects of the case which can be better considered later. Of one thing there can, however, be no doubt. When the writer to the Hebrews says, figuratively, that Jesus " suffered without the gate," he can mean nothing different from what Paul meant when he said, literally, that because Jesus was crucified he became a curse. When the writer to the Hebrews speaks of going to Jesus without the camp and bearing his reproach, he can mean nothing else than what Paul means when he speaks of being crucified with Christ. I say without hesitation that he can mean nothing else; because, if he did, we should have no school, but simply individual writers wholly independent of one another. We should have a movement apparently uniform and harmonious, but which was really the accidental result of persons who reached the same conclusion from wholly different premises. There could be but one element in the death of Christ by which he could be regarded as suffering without the gate, and as a consequence of which his followers could be urged to go to him without the camp, bearing his reproach ; and this element was the fact that the law had pronounced the crucified to be accursed. There could be but one reason why those who served the tabernacle could not be allowed to eat of the Christian altar, and that was the fact that the crucified was polluted and a pollution.

In the first sentence of the passage quoted, the writer to the Hebrews utters in unmistakable language the relation of the Christian to the law. *If those who served the Tabernacle had no right to take part in the Christian ritual, it was equally true that the Christian had no right to take part in the Jewish ritual.* The Christian and his master were together outcast. The law had uttered its final curse upon him and them. With the law, therefore, the Christian had simply nothing further to do ; neither had the law anything further to do with him. So far as the law was concerned, the Christian was, for good or for evil, free. He was like one who has been excommunicated from the Catholic church, who therefore stands outside of it. Neither its fasts nor its feasts, neither its mass nor its confessional, has any further relation to him. If he observes the ceremonial, he is none the better. If he neglects it, he is none the worse. Indeed, he cannot observe it. He is forced to neglect

it. If he should attend the mass or the confessional, he would be driven forth with indignation. The church has cast him out. Through
this act of the church he has become dead to
the church. Thus Paul could cry: "I through
the law died unto the law."[1] Paul was dead to
the law, because the law had pronounced Jesus
accursed, and Paul, accepting him as the Messiah,
shared this curse with him. Thus by the act of
the law he had become an outcast and an alien.

It will be noticed that, in the passage quoted,
the writer to the Hebrews goes a little farther
than Paul seems sometimes inclined to go. According to his view, it would appear that the
Christian had absolutely no right to take part in
the Temple service. Paul would seem sometimes
to make it simply a matter of indifference. Certainly if the account in Acts is to be accepted as
true, Paul himself went with those that were
with him to the Temple for the fulfilment of
some ceremonial.[2] If he did this to conciliate the
Jews, as so often happens in such attempts at
conciliation, the result was quite other than that
which he had planned. If this story be regarded
as doubtful, we yet find Paul exclaiming: "To

---

[1] Galatians ii. 19.   [2] Acts xxi. 26.

the Jews I became as a Jew, that I might gain
Jews."[1]   On the other hand, he exclaims : "If
ye receive circumcision, Christ will profit you
nothing."[2] If there is any difference between
Paul and the writer to the Hebrews in regard to
this matter, it is merely superficial. It does not
affect the fundamental principle which both accept. It would be simply what so often happens,
that the disciple carries out a principle more
thoroughly than his teacher.

Having reached this result, let us look back
and see how inevitable it was that Paul should
have reached it. I have in general not much
confidence in *a priori* construction of history.
In this case, however, Paul has left footmarks
by which we can learn the way that he has trav-
elled.

Paul appears first as a rigid Jew and a persecutor of the Christians. Why did he persecute
them ? If we can answer this question, the rest
of his course will become clear. Paul was a hu-
mane man. He was even tender-hearted. He
was a fair-minded and just man. We may be
sure that he would not persecute the Christians
simply because he did not like them. He would

[1] 1 Corinthians ix. 20.   [2] Galatians v. 2.

not suffer himself to be led into cruelty by a more or less conscious prejudice. He persecuted them because he felt that it was his duty to persecute them.

Now it will not help us to try to guess why he felt that it was his duty. Eighteen centuries of guessing have done very little to clear up the whole transaction. Happily Paul gives us indications enough if we will only follow them.

The question is, why Paul felt obliged to persecute the Christians. He tells us very distinctly what was the objection that the Jew urged against the Christians. He tells us that to the Jew the cross was a "stumbling-block,"[1] a "scandal." The Jew then objected to the Christians, not primarily that they accepted as the Messiah one whom the Jews generally did not accept, but that they took for the Messiah one who had been crucified. If we ask still further why they objected to this adoption as their leader of one who had been crucified, Paul tells us distinctly that in the eye of the law the crucified was accursed.[2] From a passage in the Epistle to the Corinthians, it would seem that this was the general way in which Christ was regarded by

[1] 1 Corinthians i. 23.   [2] Galatians iii. 13.

the Jews. "Wherefore," Paul writes, "I give you to understand, that no man speaking in the Spirit of God saith, Jesus is anathema; and no man can say, Jesus is Lord, but in the Holy Spirit."[1] This passage would indicate that these expressions formed the rallying cries of the two parties, — the one party crying that Jesus is anathema, the other that he is Lord. Now, since Paul has told us why Jesus was said to be anathema, we have no occasion to look for any other reason. Paul indeed himself, after he had become a Christian, still pronounced Jesus to be legally accursed; but he did not stop with this. He called him, in spite of this, or on account of this, " Lord."

To Paul the persecutor, then, Judaism had no place for the Christian, because the leader of the Christians was anathema. If we ask further, why the fact that their leader was anathema should lead him to persecute the Christians, he gives us later, in the first person, the reason. It was because they were crucified with Christ;[2] that is, the pollution that came from the cross rested also upon them. Therefore they were to be treated as polluters of the Jewish holy things.

---

[1] 1 Corinthians xii. 3.　　　　[2] Galatians ii. 20.

Thus far we have followed the indications given by Paul himself. Judaism had no place for Christians, for they were polluted by the cross of their leader. Suddenly Paul saw, or believed that he saw, the crucified one in all the glory of God. The Christian, then, was right. Paul recognized the accursed one as Lord. In the story in the Acts, he cried, "Who art thou, Lord?" [1]

What effect would this sudden transformation have upon the reasoning that we have been considering? It could have no effect. Paul had not persecuted from prejudice or caprice. He had done it because he believed that this was what the law required. He persecuted the Christians because, as he understood the law, Judaism had no place for them. His mind was too logical to change the results and methods of his thought, because his interest lay now in another direction. Judaism had no place for the Christian. Now that he was a Christian, Judaism had no place for him. The Christian shared the pollution of the cross. Now he could cry: "I have been crucified with Christ." [2] Now he felt obliged to follow his new Lord without the

[1] Acts ix. 5.   [2] Galatians ii. 20.

camp, bearing his reproach,[1] just as he had been forcing the Christians to follow him without the camp, bearing his reproach. He cast in his lot with them with as little hesitation as he had forced that lot upon them. Everything was the same now that he was a Christian that it was before. Everything was the same, and yet how different! There was a whole other side of which he had not dreamed. Before, he had urged that the Christian was crucified with Christ. Now he repeated for himself the same condemnation, but he added to it a sentence which changed its whole significance: "I have been crucified with Christ, nevertheless I live; yet not I, but Christ liveth in me."[2]

The same logic that made Paul a persecutor while he was a Jew made him preach the abrogation of the law after he became a Christian; only what from the outside looked like shame, seen from the inside was glory. What from the outside seemed banishment, seen from the inside was a home-coming to the freedom of the child.

The familiar lines which were so often on the lips of the schoolboy in my earlier years, in which

---

[1] Hebrews xiii. 13.   [2] Galatians ii. 20 f.

Catiline described the effect of his banishment, contains the logic of the whole situation. The departing Catiline exclaimed : —

> "Banished! I thank you for 't; it breaks my chain.
> I held some slack allegiance till this hour,
> But now my sword 's my own."

Thus Catiline might have said : " I through the law am dead to the law. Rome in banishing me sets me free. I am no longer a Roman, and am no longer subject to the laws of Rome." Paul had held no " slack allegiance." No more devoted servant of Judaism ever lived than he : but now he followed the guiding hand of God himself. He accepted as the Messiah one to whom God had given his glory. For so doing, the law pronounced him anathema. He accepted the judgment ; but to his surprise he found that as an exile from Judaism he entered the land of blessedness and liberty, of the possibility of which he had never dreamed.

The first result of the crucifixion to the thought of Paul was, that by it for the Christian the law was abrogated. This was an event that could not have been foreseen. In it what would have seemed the impossible became the actual. Paul regarded the law as divinely appointed. In the great change of his faith, he did not lose this confidence in the divine origin of the law. It was one of the striking facts in Paul's spiritual development that he never went backward. As we have seen before, his beliefs were carefully wrought out and their foundations were well established. He simply pressed forward and let his original beliefs develop into whatever results they would. As we have seen, the relation of the Christian to the law was to him precisely the same after his conversion that it was before ; only this relation involved consequences which before he had not suspected. In like manner his fundamental thought of the law was not changed. He simply found in the law itself utterances which implied that from the beginning it was meant to be transitory. He passed out from under the law as reverently as he had lived under it. It was through the law itself that he died to the law. No other power than that of the law itself would have released him from its authority.

The Remission of Sins.

The next result of the crucifixion, one that was involved in the one just stated, was the remission of the sins that had been committed

against the law, and the removal of the condemnation that these sins had incurred. As in
the time of the French Revolution, when the
tyranny under which France had terribly suffered was overthrown, the prisoners that were
languishing under its condemnation for crimes
committed against it came forth into the light
of liberty, so when the Jewish law was abrogated,
old scores were wiped out, and old offences lost
their condemnation. The penalties of the law
were no longer dreaded, for the law that had
imposed them had ceased to be.

All this, it will be noticed, is quite opposite
from the ordinary view of Paul's teaching. It
has been held that Christ by his death bore the
penalty of human transgressions ; that the sins
of those who trusted in him were thus remitted ;
and that on account of this, in some way which
it was impossible to make very clear, the law
was abrogated. Between these two transactions
— the remission of sins and the abrogation of
the law — there was no logical connection. According to the view here presented, the process
was the reverse of this. The law was first abrogated, and through this abrogation of the law the
sins which had been committed under it were

remitted. The connection between the two transactions is a logical and inevitable one.

However clear and obvious this relation is, the
other view has become so established by long
association that I should almost despair of finding acceptance for the one which I present, if it
were not that in the New Testament itself I find
this directly stated. As we have already seen,
the Epistle to the Colossians may be taken as
illustrating in this fundamental matter the
thought of Paul ; for if it was not written by
him, it none the less represents the school of
thought which he established. In this epistle
we read : "And you, being dead through your
trespasses and the uncircumcision of your flesh,
you, I say, did he quicken together with him, having forgiven us all our trespasses ; *having blotted
out the bond written in ordinances that was against
us, which was contrary to us : and he hath taken
it out of the way, nailing it to the cross.*" [1]   In
this passage we are distinctly told that our trespasses were forgiven, because the bond written
in ordinances, or in the alternate translation
which the Revised Version suggests, "the bond
that was against us by its ordinances," was taken

[1] Colossians ii. 13, 14.

out of the way. This is obviously and unmistakably the Jewish law. It was the law which
was nailed to the cross. In other words, the
law and the Christ came into collision. The law
condemned him and won thus a temporary victory ; but in condemning him it condemned itself. By this last act of authority it abdicated
its authority. Thus it was nailed to the cross
by a permanent crucifixion. Jesus rose glorified ; the law died eternally. The passage before us insists that the forgiveness of our trespasses was the result of the crucifixion of the
law ; that is, of its abrogation through the crucifixion of Christ, which is directly opposed to
the commonly received view. This view, I repeat, makes the forgiveness of sins primary and
the abolition of the law secondary ; while the
writer to the Colossians makes the abolition of
the law primary and the forgiveness of sins secondary. In this the writer to the Colossians
illustrates and confirms the result which we have
already reached from the study of the Pauline
epistles.

In this connection it is important to notice
that the passage which begins with the forgiveness of sins, basing this upon the abrogation of

the law, passes at once to the exhortation to the maintenance of Christian liberty : " Let no man therefore judge you in meat, or in drink, or in respect of a feast day or a new moon or a sabbath day." [1]   All this from the point of view which has been generally held seems to have little to do with the forgiveness of sins.   From that point of view the author seems to write inconsequently. From the point of view here insisted upon, the passage assumes a logical consistency.   Indeed, it is not infrequently the case that this interpretation brings order and sequence into the Pauline writing in cases where they had seemed most lacking.

The view of Paul's teaching which sees the remission of sins to have been the result of the abolition of the law receives another striking confirmation from a passage in the Epistle to the Hebrews which speaks of the death of Christ as the basis of the remission of sins that had been committed under the law.   The passage is as follows : " And for this cause he is the mediator of a new covenant, that a death having taken place *for the redemption of the transgressions that were under the first covenant,* they that

[1] Colossians ii. 16.

have been called may receive the promise of the eternal inheritance."[1]   Here we are made to understand that the redemption wrought by the death of Christ was that of transgressions under the first covenant.   "The first covenant" was obviously the Mosaic law.   It was not sin in general that was redeemed, but transgressions of the law of Moses.   All this requires much forcing to adapt it to the ordinary view of the sacrificial death of Christ.   It adapts itself, however, simply and naturally to what we have seen to be the Pauline view.

This view is further illustrated by the solemn warning given in the Epistle to the Hebrews, that no further sacrifice for sin is possible.   The passage is this : " For if we sin wilfully after that we have received the knowledge of the truth, there remaineth no more a sacrifice for sins."[2] This statement, unlike the others that I have quoted, would admit of an interpretation in accordance with the commonly received view of the Pauline theology ; and we must certainly not regard it as an application of his teaching made by Paul himself.   It conforms, however, most naturally to the view of Paul's doctrine which I

[1] Hebrews ix. 15.   [2] Hebrews x. 26.

am presenting, and is a naturally suggested de-
duction from it.   If the death of Christ was for
the remission of sins committed under the law,
it would have no relation to sins committed by
those who have been emancipated from the law.
For those who under these circumstances sinned
wilfully, there remained no more offering for sin.

Should the explanation of Paul's view of the
remission of sins by the death of Christ, namely,
that sins were remitted because the law was done
away, seem to any indirect and cold, I will call
attention to the fact that it is suggested in the
most impassioned utterance of Paul that has
come down to us.   I mean the passage in which
he cries : "O death, where is thy victory ?   O
death, where is thy sting ?   The sting of death
is sin ; and the power of sin is the law : but
thanks be to God, which giveth us the victory
through our Lord Jesus Christ." [1]   In this passage, the idea that the power of sin is lost because the law is done away fits perfectly with the
passion of the outburst ; while the explanation
commonly given, that the law loses its power
because in the substitutionary death of Christ its
demands were met, is awkward and far-fetched.

[1] 1 Corinthians xv. 55–57.

Salvation for the Gentiles.

The question now presses : What part had the Gentiles in all this ? What effect did the abolition of the law have upon them ? How could the death of Christ be in any sense regarded as the propitiation for their sins when, being wholly outside the law, they had not sinned against it ? Now and then, however, we find it so spoken of. Thus in the Epistle of John we read : "He is the propitiation for our sins ; and not for ours only, but also for the whole world." [1]

Though the Gentile was not under the law, he was under the shadow of it. The Gentile was, as Paul insists, also a sinner.[2] To the Jew the law was the vehicle of a promise. The Gentile had no part in this promise. For him there was no hope. When the law was annulled, however, the promise which had been wrapped up in it remained in its fulness, and for the first time appeared in its beauty. By the annulling of the law the limitation which had excluded the Gentile from the hope of Israel was done away. The Jew had become as the Gentile and the Gentile had thereby become as the Jew.

[1] I John ii. 2.   [2] Romans i. 18–32, *et passim.*

It is fortunate that in regard to each of the most important aspects of the atoning death of Christ we find in the New Testament at least one luminous passage which makes clear the whole matter. The classical passage in regard to the relation of the death of Christ to the Gentile world is found in the second chapter of the Epistle to the Ephesians. There we read: "Wherefore remember, that aforetime ye, the Gentiles in the flesh, who are called Uncircumcision by that which is called Circumcision, in the flesh, made by hands; that ye were at that time separate from Christ, alienated from the commonwealth of Israel, and strangers from the covenants of the promise, having no hope and without God in the world. But now in Christ Jesus ye that once were far off are made nigh in the blood of Christ. For he is our peace, who made both one, and brake down the middle wall of partition, having abolished in his flesh the enmity, even the law of commandments contained in ordinances; that he might create in himself of the twain one new man, so making peace; and might reconcile them both in one body unto God through the cross, having slain the enmity thereby: and he came and preached peace to you that were far off, and peace to them that were nigh : for through him we both have our access in one Spirit unto the Father. So then ye are no more strangers and sojourners, but ye are fellow-citizens with the saints, and of the household of God, being built upon the foundation of the apostles and prophets, Christ Jesus himself being the chief corner-stone." [1]

In this passage we see that the central thought is that Christ abolished in his flesh the law of commandments contained in ordinances. Through this abolition of the law the middle wall of partition between the Jew and the Gentile was broken down, and the enmity between Jew and Gentile was done away. Before, the Gentiles had no hope and were without God in the world ; but now, through this abolition of the law, they had become fellow-citizens with the saints and of the household of God.

All this, like other parts of Paul's gospel, has a positive side. We are here considering only such expressions as refer to the remission of sins, and to Christ as the propitiation, and thus the means of such remission. By his death the past of the Gentile as well as the past of the Jew had been

[1] Ephesians ii. 11–20.

done away. The Gentile, like the Jew, had become a new man. Each started afresh, freed from the old condemnation, and each was thus ready for the new life which came through Christ. Each could form a part in a holy temple of the Lord in whom all were builded together for a habitation of God in the spirit.

Figurative Language.

From the view held by Paul and his followers in regard to the death of Christ, it follows very naturally that this death should be spoken of as a sacrifice. We have already seen that sacrificial language when applied to the death of Christ carries with it no presumption in favor of the traditional theory that in his death Christ bore directly, in any sense, the penalty of man's sin. The presumption is wholly in the other direction.[1] We have now to notice that this sacrificial language is obviously figurative.   There was on Calvary no sacrifice in the technical sense. There was no priest and no altar.   The figure was, however, one that was most naturally suggested.   It was based upon two points of resemblance.   One of these was the presence of a slain

[1] See chapter i.

victim ; the other was that through the death of
this victim forgiveness of sins was granted to
those who put their trust in it. As we have
already seen, the figure gives no hint as to the
manner in which, according to the thought of
Paul, the death of the victim accomplished this
result.

The purely figurative use of the sacrificial terms
that are applied to the death of Christ is very
clearly illustrated by the manner in which these
terms are used in the Epistle to the Hebrews.
In this epistle the treatment is peculiarly transparent. In the ninth chapter there is a passage
which is important in this respect, to which reference has been made in another place.[1] Here
the strongest sacrificial language is used, and
this is immediately followed by an explanation
of the sense in which it is to be understood. The
passage is as follows : " For if the blood of goats
and bulls, and the ashes of a heifer sprinkling
them that have been defiled, sanctify unto the
cleanness of the flesh : how much more shall the
blood of Christ, who through the eternal Spirit
offered himself without blemish unto God, *cleanse
your conscience from dead works to serve the living*

[1] Hebrews ix. 13–15. See p. 133 f.

God ? " Here the cleansing the conscience from dead works obviously refers to the abolition of the law by the death of Christ. Indeed, the object of the epistle is to illustrate this emancipation and the new life that was united with it. This spiritual freedom is what is referred to in the sometimes misunderstood passage with which the sixth chapter opens :[1] " Wherefore let us cease to speak of the first principles of Christ, and press on unto perfection ; not laying again a foundation of repentance from dead works, and of faith toward God, of the teaching of baptisms, and of laying on of hands, and of resurrection of the dead, and of eternal judgment. And this will we do, if God permit." All that is here left behind, not as worthless but as first principles already established, was common to both branches of the early church. The perfection to which the writer would press on is the Pauline doctrine of the emancipation from the law by the death of Christ. This result of Christ's death the writer commends to the Jewish readers by sacrificial language, which, however, as in the case before us, he is careful to explain. The most striking illustrations of the anti-Jewish tendency of the

[1] Hebrews vi. 1–3.

epistle is the comparison of Melchizedek and Christ, which will be spoken of later : and the saying in the last chapter in regard to the altar "whereof they have no right to eat which serve the tabernacle," which has been already referred to.[1]

Another passage in which the writer to the Hebrews makes clear the sense in which he uses sacrificial language in regard to the death of Christ is found in the tenth chapter of the epistle. It is as follows : " For by one offering he hath perfected forever them that are sanctified. And the Holy Ghost also beareth witness to us : for after he hath said,

> This is the covenant that I will make with them
> After those days, saith the Lord ;
> I will put my laws on their heart,
> And upon their mind also will I write them ;

then saith he,

> And their sins and their iniquities will I remember no more.

Now where remission of these is, there is no more offering for sin." [2]

In this passage the word "perfected," which occurs at its opening, is hardly in conformity

---

[1] Hebrews xiii 10.   See p. 148 f.

[2] Hebrews x. 14–18 ; Jeremiah xxxi. 33 f.

with a strict use of the sacrificial figure. The
language of the quotation from the prophet which
speaks of putting the divine laws upon the heart
and writing them upon the mind, the author evidently understands as prophetic of the abolition
of the Mosaic law and the spiritual freedom of
the Christian. The last clauses show in what
sense the sacrificial figure is used. Since through
the death of Christ there is remission of sins, this
death takes the place of sacrifices, and these, for
the Christian, cease forever.

The quotation just made not only illustrates
the fact that sacrificial language, when used in
connection with the death of Christ, has a figurative sense, but also the fact that the sacrificial
figure is used very loosely. A further example
of this looseness is found in the fact that Christ
is spoken of both as priest and victim. Other
figures besides that of sacrifice are also used to
describe the atoning effect of the death of
Christ. The idea of redemption is frequently
used in this connection. Thus we read, "In
whom we have our redemption through his blood,
the forgiveness of our trespasses." [1] The idea
of a testament which is ineffective before the

[1] Ephesians i. 7.

death of the testator is used to express the same
thing. In the ninth chapter of the Epistle to
the Hebrews we have all these figures used in
the same presentation.[1] First, we read of a
death having taken place for the redemption of
the sins that were under the first covenant."
In explanation it is said, " For where a testament
is, there must of necessity be the death of him
who made it." After the idea of the death of a
testator had been dwelt upon, the passage proceeds: " Wherefore, even the first covenant hath
not been dedicated without blood." Then follows an account of the use of blood in instituting
the first covenant, and the passage closes : " And
according to the law, I may almost say, all things
are cleansed with blood, and apart from the shedding of blood there is no remission." Here we
have the fact that a will is of no effect before
the death of the testator, placed as the connect-
ing link between the statement that the redemption of the sins under the first covenant was
accomplished by a death, and the statement of
the necessity of the shedding of sacrificial blood
for the remission of sins ; the connection being
indicated in the one case by the particle " for,"

[1] Hebrews ix. 15–22.

and in the other by a "therefore." Of these figures, the one taken from the facts in regard to a
will is the least to the point. Its presence with
the others shows, however, how loosely these are
taken. The others, indeed, — that which involves
the idea of redemption and that based upon sacrifice, — are so closely allied that they might
easily be used in the same connection. The idea
of the testament is wholly foreign to them.

Another figure which is used to illustrate the
freedom from the law that was accomplished by
the death of Christ is that of divorce by death.
This is urged by Paul in the seventh chapter of
the Epistle to the Romans.[1] It is a figure which
has little significance for the traditional interpretation of Paul's teaching, but which has great
pertinence when we reach his real thought. The
presentation of the figure is confused. The wife
is said to be freed from legal obligation to her
husband by his death. The Christian is freed
from bondage to the law by his own death to it.
This confusion is, however, superficial and verbal.
After the death of the husband, the wife, so far
as legal obligations are concerned, might be said
to be dead to him. Paul might have spoken with

[1] Romans vii. 1–6.

propriety of the law as dead. This was doubtless what was in his mind. In the Epistle to the Colossians, as we have seen, the law is spoken of as crucified. There we read of "the bond written in ordinances that was against us," that God "hath taken it out of the way, nailing it to the cross."[1] Paul's thought in the figure based upon marriage and divorce is that the law being dead the believer cannot be condemned for uniting himself to "him who was raised from the dead." It was probably for the sake of greater ease of expression that the figure was, perhaps unconsciously, superficially changed.

The figure used by Paul in the opening of the sixth chapter of the Epistle to the Romans, based upon the idea of being buried with Christ in baptism and rising with him to newness of life, does not demand our present consideration, as it represents an aspect of the Christian life quite different from that which we are at present considering.

The looseness with which the sacrificial figure is used may be further illustrated by the fact that sacrificial terms are applied not merely to the death of Christ, but to other aspects of the

[1] Colossians ii. 14.

Christian's relation to God.   These varied appli-
cations stand often in close connection with one
another.   The passage in the thirteenth chapter
of the Epistle to the Hebrews, which compares
Christ to the sacrificial victim which was burned
without the camp, proceeds : " Through him then
let us offer up a sacrifice of praise to God continually, that is, the fruit of lips which make
confession to his name.   But to do good and to
communicate forget not : for with such sacrifices
God is well pleased." [1]

2 *Corinthians* v. 21.

We have thus far considered chiefly such passages in the writings of Paul and his followers
as were suited to make clear his central and fundamental thought.   We have now to consider
certain more abstract statements of Paul which
assume in the reader a knowledge of the essential elements of his teaching.   The other passages state definitely Paul's thought.   We have
to use the result thus reached to throw light
upon those that are more obscure.   In this application of our result we have a test of its truth.
If where the current view of Paul's doctrine

[1] Hebrews xiii. 15, 16.

introduces only confusion, the view that I am urging brings clearness and simplicity, the truth of this view will receive the best confirmation.

The principal passage that we have thus to consider is the great and central statement found in Romans iii. 24–26. Before studying this, however, we will turn to one that is simpler but no less important. The passage to which I refer is the twenty-first verse of the fifth chapter of the Second Epistle to the Corinthians : " Him who knew no sin he made to be sin on our behalf ; that we might become the righteousness of God in him." In connection with this verse we read in Meyer's Commentary [1] as follows : " It is to be noted . . . that ἁμαρτίαν, just like κατάρα, Gal. iii. 13, includes in itself the notion of guilt ; further, that the guilt of which Christ, made to be sin and a curse by God, appears as bearer was not his own (μὴ γνόντα ἁμαρτίαν), and that hence the guilt of *men* who through his death were to be justified by God was *transferred* to him ; consequently the justification of men is *imputative.*" I do not know that there is anything in the passage before us which would necessarily forbid this interpretation. It is different with the passage in the

[1] In a note.

Epistle to the Galatians to which the critic refers. If the words "who knew no sin" in the Epistle to the Corinthians might suggest imputation, the words of Galatians iii. 13 exclude this notion. There, as we have seen, Christ is accursed, not on account of the sins of others, but on account of the situation in which he was himself placed. He was accursed because he himself was crucified. The critic is right in using one of these passages to throw light upon the other, but the comparison leads to a result very different from that reached by him. The verse from the Epistle to the Galatians makes impossible the interpretation given to the verse from the Epistle to the Corinthians. Even without this comparison, the interpretation just cited is a far-fetched one. If there is nothing in the passage to forbid it, there is nothing to justify it.

When the two passages, 2 Corinthians v. 21 and Galatians iii. 13, are compared, with no complication with traditional theories, and with no assumption of anything which the passages do not contain, the result is very simple. In the Epistle to the Galatians we read that Christ was made a curse through being crucified. In the Epistle to the Galatians we read that though he

knew no sin, yet he was made sin. In the light
of the former passage these words lose even the
air of paradox. In himself, in his life, Christ did
not know sin. In his death on the cross he "was
made sin." This was not by imputation, but by
his own position. We see the special apposite-
ness of the words "was made *sin*." He was not
made a *sinner*. He had committed no sin. He
was not even put in the place of the sinner. He
was made "sin" and a "curse" because the law
pronounces the crucified to be accursed.

Romans iii. 24–26.

We are now ready to consider that great statement of Paul to which I have already referred,
and which might almost be regarded as the text
of this whole discussion. It is as follows : "Being justified freely by his grace through the redemption that is in Christ Jesus : whom God
set forth to be a propitiation, through faith, by
his blood, to show his righteousness, because of
the passing over of the sins done aforetime, in
the forbearance of God ; for the showing, I say,
of his righteousness at this present season : that
he might himself be just, and the justifier of him
that hath faith in Jesus."

This passage has too often been made the starting-point in the discussion of Paul's doctrine of the atonement. It should stand at the conclusion of such a discussion rather than at the beginning. Taken by itself, it is extremely large and vague. If the idea of sacrifice carried with it, as it has been so often supposed to do, the notion of a transferrence of penalty from the sinner to the victim, then the word "propitiation" might suggest something definite in regard to the nature of the efficacy of the death of Christ. Since the idea of sacrifice had, as we have seen, no such meaning, the passage, taken by itself, offers no hint of its significance. I suppose that it is this very vagueness which has made it so attractive to many. It affords great freedom for speculation. Theories and fancies have made their nests in it, like rooks in some old tower.

In approaching the consideration of this passage, it is important to consider first the structure of the sentence, and to observe the formal relation of its parts to one another. The sentence is very long and involved ; but at the heart of it we find two statements which are very closely connected. They both undertake to show

why God set forth Christ Jesus to be a propitiation. One of these says that it was "to show
his righteousness, because of the passing over
of the sins done aforetime." The second goes
back to the important word "righteousness,"
and, starting afresh from that, states that the
propitiation was accomplished that God "might
be just and the justifier of him that hath faith
in Jesus." The relation between these two
members of the sentence to one another is, in
our English translation, clearly expressed by the
words "*I say*," which the translators introduced
in order that the connection might be readily
perceived. Any one looking at these clauses
from the outside, and having little or no knowledge of the thought of Paul, would naturally
assume that the two clauses express the same
thought; the one saying under one form what
the other says under another. The construction of the sentence would seem to imply that
Paul stated an idea, and then, for some reason,
made a restatement of the same thought. All
the commentators whom I have consulted take,
however, a different view of the passage. While
the second of the clauses under consideration
refers in so many words to the justification of

those who believe in Christ, the former of them is made by these commentators to refer to the sins that had been committed in the world before the appearance of Christ.   Meyer explains that the transaction was " on account of the passing by of sins that had previously taken place, *i. e.*, because He [God] had allowed the pre-Christian sins to go without punishment, whereby His righteousness had been lost sight of and obscured, and therefore came to need an ἔνδειξις for men.   Thus the atonement accomplished in Christ became the divine ' Theodicée for the past history of the world ' (Tholuck)."

The weight of authority is so strong in favor of this construction, that if it were a matter to be determined by technical scholarship, I, for one, should not dare to question it.   It is, however, not a matter of translation but one of interpretation ; and the interpretation that has just been given is connected with a view of the general teaching of Paul which I believe to be false.   We therefore need not hesitate to consider it on its merits.

The common interpretation is met by objections, each one of which is serious, and which taken together appear to me to be fatal.

In the first place, this interpretation makes the sentence incoherent and self-contradictory. It makes Paul give two reasons for the same trans-action, and to give them as if they were one rea-son. The first of the two clauses makes the transaction look backward, the second makes it look forward. Now the same transaction may easily involve these two aspects; but the diffi-culty is that this interpretation makes Paul give the two as though they were one and the same. Perhaps I can best make the point clear by an illustration. In the time of the war with Mexico patriotic orators were in the habit of exclaiming, "We are fighting to secure indemnity for the past and security for the future." I do not be-lieve that any speaker, unless possibly some after-dinner orator, ever exclaimed, "We are fighting for indemnity for the past; fighting, I say, for security for the future." Yet it is precisely such incoherent eloquence which the interpretation under consideration ascribes to Paul.

A second objection is that this interpretation introduces a subject which is wholly foreign to the matter of Paul's discourse. In verses 21 and 22 he stated the theme which he proposed to consider. He says : "But now apart from the

law a righteousness of God hath been manifested,
. . . even the righteousness through faith in Jesus
Christ unto all them that believe." This theme
he presents through all the rest of the chapter.
The interpretation we are considering, however,
makes him pause in his fervid eloquence, and
turn aside to contemplate for a moment something that concerned pre-Christian times. After
this digression he turns back to the course of
thought that he had been following.

In the third place, the thought thus introduced
is in absolute contradiction to what Paul had
been saying in the earlier part of the epistle.
Paul had been speaking of the terrors of the law.
He had said : " For the wrath of God is revealed
from heaven against all ungodliness and unrighteousness of men." [1] He had exclaimed to the
sinner, that he was treasuring up for himself
" wrath in the day of wrath and revelation of the
righteous judgment of God." [2] He had said that
unto them that "obey unrighteousness shall be
wrath and indignation, tribulation and anguish,
upon every soul of man that worketh evil." [3]
He had said : " For as many as have sinned
without law shall also perish without law : and

[1] Romans i. 18.   [2] Romans ii. 5.   [3] Romans ii. 8 f.

as many as have sinned under law shall be judged by law." [1] Yet in the face of all this, the common interpretation makes Paul imply that, on account of the mildness and remissness of God in the past a " theodicy " was needed. The only theodicy that would be in keeping with these awful utterances of Paul was that of the judgment day.

It is beside the mark to refer in this connection to the words that are put into Paul's mouth in the book of Acts. There he is made to speak of an overlooking of sins in the past. In the expressive language of King James's version, he is represented as saying : " And the times of this ignorance God winked at." [2] These elaborate speeches in the book of Acts cannot, under the most favorable judgment, be regarded as literal statements of what the speakers actually said. Further, if Paul did say this, it would throw no light on the passage before us, where the whole course of the thought is different. As, however, this passage has been cited in connection with that now under consideration from the Epistle to the Romans, attention may be called to its harmony with the view of the latter that I am

---

[1] Romans ii. 12.   [2] Acts xvii. 30.

urging.   When I said, a few lines back, that the only theodicy which Paul's words would allow was that of the judgment day, I did not have in mind this passage in the book of Acts : "The times of ignorance therefore God overlooked ; but now he commandeth men that they should all everywhere repent : inasmuch as he hath appointed a day, in the which he will judge the world." [1]   According to this statement laxity is followed by the judgment.   The whole passage should, however, be left out of the account in this discussion.

We must assume, then, that the two clauses which we have been considering say the same thing in different forms ; that the words "righteousness" (δικαιοσύνης) and "just" (δίκαιον) not only refer to the same quality, but that their application is to the same persons.   Paul first says : "Whom God set forth to be a propitiation, through faith, by his blood, to show his righteousness, because of the passing over of the sins done-aforetime, in the forbearance of God." This, however, is an abstract statement.   It gives the object of the transaction in a general way, suggesting the principle of the thing, but not its

[1] Acts xvii. 30, 31.

direct application. He therefore goes back and starts afresh with the principal word of the statement just referred to, in order to say precisely whose were the sins that were thus passed over. He goes on : " For the showing, I say, of his righteousness at this present season ; that He might himself be just and the justifier of him that hath faith in Jesus."

This is the construction which the form of the sentence seems peremptorily to require, and the forsaking of which involves, as we have seen, many difficulties. The difficulties which this construction may suggest to any reader, I hope will disappear when we consider the real meaning of the passage.

Passing from the consideration of the formal relation of the clauses of the passage to one another, we have now to seek its substantial meaning.

The first question that meets us is as to the relation between this passage and the statements that are made by Paul in his Epistle to the Galatians, which we have before considered.

We here fall back upon certain assumptions that were made by us in entering upon this general discussion.[1] These assumptions were in

[1] Pages 197 ff.

effect that, unless there were reasons to the contrary, wherever Paul speaks of the objective aspect of the atonement he must be considered to mean substantially the same thing, and that the more concrete statements should be used to explain those that are more abstract. According to these assumptions, we should explain this passage, which is extremely abstract, by the statements in the second and third chapters of the Epistle to the Galatians.

This course was, as I have intimated, to be followed in case there were no insuperable objections. Do such objections exist in the present case ? Professor Lipsius, in his commentary on the passage, insists that such objections do exist. He says : " Notice that here only the sacrificial quality of the blood of Christ is made prominent, while there is no reference to the manner of the death, the death on the cross." If we must be as literal as this, we shall have to meet still other complications. Paul elsewhere says that, "We were reconciled to God by the death of his Son." [1] In this passage neither the cross nor the blood is referred to. If the principle of Lipsius is to be applied in one case, there is no reason why it

[1] Romans v. 10.

should not be applied in all cases. We should then have three different aspects of the objective efficiency of the death of Christ ; one, in which the death itself should be the effective element, as in the theory of Saint Anselm and of Dr. Cave ; another, in which the blood should be the effective element; this might possibly signify violence and consequent suffering, according to the theory of Dr. Shedd ; or it might refer to its sacrificial character, which in this case would not be recognized in " the death." The third would refer to the death upon the cross. Yet, further, Paul reminds the Ephesians that God in Christ hath forgiven them.[1] In this passage we would seem to have an atonement from which the death and the blood and the cross are alike excluded. We should then have a fourth aspect of the atonement.

How much simpler is it to assume that Paul in all these cases meant the same thing. This is not only simpler, it is more reasonable. Jesus died only once, and that was on the cross. His blood was shed only once, and that was upon the cross. It is reasonable, therefore, to assume that when the death of Christ is spoken of, Paul

[1] Ephesians iv. 32.

means his death as it actually occurred, namely,
his death on the cross. When his blood is referred to, it is reasonable to suppose that Paul
means his blood as it was actually shed, that is,
on the cross. We may illustrate this by the
manner in which the ordinary sacrificial victim
is spoken of. The writer to the Hebrews speaks
of "the blood of goats and bulls" as sanctifying
"unto the cleanness of the flesh."[1] The blood
of bulls and of goats was never believed to have
in itself any cleansing efficacy. The blood that
was shed in the shambles was valueless. It was
the blood that was shed under special circumstances, namely, according to the appointed rites
of the sacrifice, which had power. As the blood
of the bull or the goat was taken to represent
the concrete whole of the sacrifice with the altar
and the solemn rites, so the blood of Christ
should be taken as representing the concrete
whole which included all the circumstances of
his death. As the blood of the victim had no
atoning force except as shed amid the sanctities
of the temple, so it is natural to assume that the
blood of Christ had no atoning efficacy, except
as it was shed in the midst of the pollution of
the cross.

[1] Hebrews ix. 13.

The manner in which different aspects of the
event are used by the New Testament writers
to express the same relation may be specially
illustrated by a statement made in the Epistle
to the Ephesians. Here we read : " But now in
Christ Jesus ye that once were far off are made
nigh in the blood of Christ." [1] This whole passage is unmistakably speaking of the adoption of
the Gentiles into the sweep of the divine promises, because the " middle wall of partition," by
which we are told is meant " the law of commandments contained in ordinances," was broken
down by Christ. The blood of Christ is thus
used to express the efficiency of the crucifixion
in regard to the doing away of the law. Associations with other interpretations may make
the passage Romans iii. 25 appear to some to
have a different meaning. In regard to the passage which I just quoted from the Epistle to the
Ephesians, there can be no doubt. We are told
in it, in so many words, that it refers to the doing away of the law. That is precisely what
Paul tells us in the Epistle to the Galatians was
accomplished by the curse which the law pronounced upon the crucified.[2] He there says that

[1] Ephesians ii. 13.   [2] Galatians iii. 13 f.

Christ by his crucifixion was made a curse for us, "that upon the Gentiles might come the blessing of Abraham in Christ Jesus." In these two passages, then, we have the abolition of the law spoken of. In one the blood of Christ, and in the other the cross of Christ, is referred to as accomplishing this result.

In fact, all the expressions that have been referred to, as well as others, seem to be used by Paul to express the same central fact. Sometimes it is that Christ was delivered up for us all.[1] Sometimes it is that in him we are forgiven.[2] Sometimes the death of Christ,[3] sometimes his blood,[4] sometimes his crucifixion is specified.[5] So far as these expressions refer to the objective aspect of the atonement accomplished by the death of Christ, there is no reason to doubt that they all mean substantially the same thing. Sometimes Paul would seem to take one or the other word simply because it was the one that happened to come into his mind. There is sometimes, however, evidently a reason for the use of one of these terms rather than another. In the passages before us, Romans iii. 25, and Ga-

[1] Romans viii. 32.   [2] Ephesians iv. 32.   [3] Romans v. 10.
[4] Romans v. 9.   [5] Galatians iii. 13.

latians iii. 13, there is an obvious reason why the
blood of Christ is referred to in the one case,
and the cross in the other. To the Galatians
Paul was speaking literally. He feared that they
were being drawn away from the gospel that
he had preached to them, and he wished to re-
mind them of the arguments by which his teaching was supported. He therefore tells them
outright in what manner the cross was the means
of doing away with the law and of introducing
the consequent higher life of the spirit. In
writing to the Romans, Paul was not arguing, and
he assumed that his readers understood what
he was talking about. If they had not known
this in advance, the passage would have been as
meaningless to them as it has been to later generations. Moreover, in this passage Paul is speaking figuratively. He is comparing Jesus to the
sacrificial victim.[1] I suppose that it will not be

[1] "ἱλαστήριον cannot stand for a means of atonement in general. This is too vague. The word θῦμα must be understood."
Lipsius' *Commentary*, a. l.

It should be stated that Lipsius does not accept the view that
the sacrificial victim among the Hebrews was punished in the
place of the sinner. In the Hebrew sacrifice he sees " a covering of the sinner and of his guilt before the eyes of God
through the blood of the sacrifice, by which the offerer mani-

contended that this language is not figurative.
Put what meaning we will into the death of
Christ, we cannot make of his death a literal sacrifice.[1] It might take the place of a sacrifice,
but it was not a sacrifice in any literal or ordinary meaning of the term. Paul was too good a
rhetorician to say that " God set forth " Christ
Jesus "to be a propitiation upon the cross ;" for
the sacrificial victim was not crucified. What
he says is, that he was set forth to be a propitiation in, or by means of, his blood ; and thus
the picture is complete. From his youth the
bloody sacrifice must have impressed Paul more
than almost anything beside. The image of the
slain Christ must have haunted with equal vividness his imagination. Since the death of Christ
practically accomplished what the death of the

---

fests his recognition of the fact that he deserves punishment."
On the other hand, Weiss, in the eighth edition of Meyer's *Commentary on the Romans*, urges that ἱλαστήριον signifies a means
of atonement in general. This seems to me to take all special
meaning out of the passage, and leaves the words " in his blood "
without definite application. While, however, in the text I accept the position of Lipsius in regard to this word, the difference
is of no importance so far as my general interpretation of Paul's
teaching is concerned.

[1] Compare pp. 168 ff.

sacrificial victim was meant to accomplish, it is not strange that the two flowed together and formed one picture to his thought.

What has just been said gains additional force when we notice that the whole framework of the thought in which the passage in the Epistle to the Romans that we are considering has its place is precisely that in which the verses from the Epistle to the Galatians which we have considered have their place. In both epistles Paul urges the hopelessness of salvation under the law. To the Romans he said : " By the works of the law shall no flesh be justified." [1] To the Galatians he said : " Now that no man is justified by the law in the sight of God, is evident." [2] To both he was insisting that through Christ the believer escaped from the power of the law. To the Romans he said : " But now apart from the law a righteousness of God hath been manifested." [3] To the Galatians he said that Christ " redeemed us from the curse of the law." [4] In both cases there was the same problem to be solved, namely, to honor the law while setting it aside. In the Epistle to the Romans the word

[1] Romans iii. 20.   [2] Galatians iii. 11.
[3] Romans iii. 21.   [4] Galatians iii. 13.

righteousness, δικαιοσύνη, is used, as the best commentators insist, in a forensic sense. It signifies
the giving to the law the honor which is its due.
It will be noticed that the propitiation is not set
forth in order that sins before committed may
be passed over, or in order that the believer may
be justified. All this is, in the passage, taken
for granted. It was implied in the promise to
Abraham, as Paul elsewhere tells us, that the
believer was to be accepted without regard to
the law.[1] The righteousness of God was to be
shown *on account of* this passing over of former
sins. He was to be just *while* justifying the believer. In other words, the law was to be honored even while it was annulled. With a like significance Paul exclaims : " I *through the law* died
unto the law." [2] Putting the two passages together, we reach the result that God shows his
righteousness, that is, his respect for the law, or
as we should say in regard to men, his obedience
to the law, by making the law itself the instrument of its own annulment. How this is accomplished Paul tells us in the thirteenth verse of
the third chapter of the Epistle to the Galatians.

[1] Compare Galatians iii. 8, *et passim*.

[2] Galatians ii. 19.

Christ by his crucifixion undergoes the curse of
the law. He becomes legally polluted. Thus he
and his followers are made free of the law by
becoming outcasts from it, and, as we have seen
elsewhere, are made free from the condemnation
of the sins that had been committed under the
law. Thus, as we might have expected, we find
the two passages saying substantially the same
thing.

It is important to notice the precise phraseology that is used by Paul in regard to the propitiation that was in Christ. It was to show the
righteousness of God on account of the passing
over of the sins done aforetime. This passing
over ($\pi\acute{a}\rho\epsilon\sigma\iota\nu$) is an expression that obviously could
not be applied to the forgiveness of sins for which
Christ had made atonement, as this atonement
has been generally understood. It is probably
this difficulty, arising from the general view that
they had adopted, which has led the commentators to unite in making the word refer to the
pre-Christian sins of the world. We have seen
into what a jungle of contradictions this expla-,
nation leads. Here the interpretation that I am
urging comes to our relief. The basis of this
may be illustrated by the passage in the Epistle

to the Colossians that has been already referred to. The Colossians were told that when "the bond written in ordinances that was against us" was "blotted out," being "nailed to the cross," the "trespasses" that had been committed against it were "forgiven."[1] In other words, the sins that had been committed against the law were suffered to lapse when the law, so far as the Christian was concerned, was done away. This is what Paul in the Epistle to the Romans naturally speaks of as "the passing over of the sins done aforetime, in the forbearance of God." No words could be chosen that would more accurately express the nature of the transaction as I have endeavored to explain it. This is to be understood, as the parallelism of the passage would indicate, as being the same thing that is later in the sentence spoken of as the justifying of the believer in Jesus. Thus, here as elsewhere, the interpretation of Paul's thought that I suggest enables us to take his language in its most literal meaning; and by following this literal meaning we escape the contradictions and difficulties that beset every other form of exposition.

[1] Colossians ii. 14.

The only objection that occurs to me as possibly to be urged against the general view that has been taken grows out of the special fitness of it to the passage in Romans that we have been examining. The phrase "passing over" ($\pi\acute{a}\rho\epsilon\sigma\iota\nu$) is so exceedingly appropriate to the allowing offences to lapse when the law against which they had been committed is done away, that one might wonder how, under these circumstances, such sins could ever be spoken of, as Paul often speaks of them, as forgiven. Though the expression in the verse under consideration is, technically speaking, the most fitting, yet it is obvious that sins that are passed over by forbearance might easily be said to be forgiven. The passage just referred to from the Epistle to the Colossians, however, removes all difficulty. In this the sins are said to be forgiven because the law had been "blotted out" and "taken away." Whatever we may think of this use of the term, we find it here so used ; and for the ends of the interpreter this is enough.

The Resurrection of Christ.

It does not need a very close examination of Paul's teaching to see that he took an entirely different view of the resurrection of Christ from that which has been taken in the later church. Modern Christians are in the habit of seeing in the resurrection of Christ the great proof of life after death. They feel that the importance of this occurrence consists in the fact that it gave visible and tangible proof that death is not the end of the life of the spirit. Certainly, it naturally lends itself to this use. To those who believe in the continued existence of the soul after death, the resurrection of Christ furnishes a most striking confirmation of this belief. What concerns us here is that to Paul it ordinarily meant something very different from this. Paul was a Pharisee, and had believed in the resurrection of the dead long before he became a Christian. He needed not the resurrection of Christ to teach him this lesson. With his Gentile converts it was different. The life after death had been, indeed, held by all peoples of whom we have knowledge from time immemorial. This belief did not, however, involve that of the resurrection; and even this had been fading out to a greater or less extent among the later Greeks and Romans. It is not strange, therefore, that some among the Corinthians should deny that there is any resurrection of the dead. To these Paul holds up the fact of the resurrection of Christ. Probably he meant, in part, to be understood as reasoning from this fact of a single resurrection to the reality of a general resurrection. He says : " Now if Christ is preached that he hath been raised from the dead, how say some among you that there is no resurrection of the dead ? " [1] This is, however, only a small part of his plea. He reasons not so much, as a modern preacher would do, from the resurrection of Christ as to this resurrection. He is not so much seeking a basis in fact for the belief in a general resurrection, as showing the momentous results that would spring from its denial. This is evident from the fact that he says not merely " if there is no resurrection of the dead, neither hath Christ been raised ; " [2] but hurries on to show what would ensue if faith in the resurrection of Christ were given up. The whole argument culminates in the saying, " If Christ hath not been raised, your faith is vain ; ye are yet in your sins." [3] The form of his reasoning thus truly represents its substance. Where the modern preacher urges, " If

[1] 1 Corinthians xv. 12.   [2] 1 Corinthians xv. 13.
[3] 1 Corinthians xv. 17.

Christ hath not been raised, there is no reason to believe in the continued life of the dead," Paul exclaimed, "For if the dead are not raised, neither hath Christ been raised." Indeed, his thought anticipates the whole attitude of the modern world towards this occurrence. To those at the present day who do not believe in a general resurrection, Christ is not risen. Thus, in an editorial article in a recent number of the "Andover Review," we read as follows : "If one has overcome the difficulty of belief in personal immortality and holds it as true that the individual survives death, why should it be incredible that Jesus survived death and gave some crowning proof of the victory in keeping with the divine life which preceded his crucifixion ?" [1] Here the reasoning is from the general belief to belief in Christ's resurrection. The writer says, however, in the same article : "Here also the question could be asked, how, if God would convince men of the reality of life beyond death, He could do it more surely than through that resurrection which abolished death ?" Here the reasoning is in the opposite direction ; as, indeed, we meet indications of this double process in Paul himself.

[1] *Andover Review*, October, 1892, p. 399.

It is not our purpose, however, to consider the general relations in which the thought of the resurrection of Christ stands to Christian theology, nor even to consider the question whether the belief in this resurrection had a basis in fact. We have simply to discover the place that it filled in the thought of Paul.

As I have said, the resurrection of Christ did not stand to Paul himself, in any degree, as a proof of a general resurrection. He needed no such proof. It was to him an occasion of joy and triumph ; not because it strengthened his faith in the future of himself and of man in general, but because it was the beginning of the great consummation. Christ was "the firstfruits of them that are asleep." [1] Persons inclosed in a beleaguered city, who may have had absolutely certain knowledge that an army is to come to their relief, may yet be pardoned if they have a special outburst of joy when they first hear the distant roar of the cannon that tells them that their deliverers have arrived. It was with such an outburst of the joy of a faith, the realization of which has actually begun, that Paul exclaimed :

[1] Corinthians xv. 20, 23.

"Now hath Christ been raised from the dead, the firstfruits of them that are asleep." [1]

Further, Paul saw in Christ the power by which the general resurrection was to be accomplished. "As in Adam all die," he exclaimed, "so also in Christ shall all be made alive." [2]   We cannot wonder at the exuberance of his joy, as he saw the beginning of the great event which was so soon to become completed, and the presence of the power that was to bring about the consummation.

The joy with which the resurrection of Christ was hailed by Paul as the forerunner of the general resurrection formed, however, only the smallest part of its interest for him.   It had a profound relation to the atoning work of Christ. Paul says of Christ that he "was delivered up for our trespasses, and was raised for our justification." [3]   Or, as we could translate with less danger of misconception, he "was delivered up on account of our trespasses, and was raised on account of our justification."   To the Corinthians he writes: "If Christ hath not been raised, your faith is vain; ye are yet in your sins." [4]

[1] 1 Corinthians xv. 20.   [2] 1 Corinthians xv. 22.
[3] Romans iv. 25.   [4] 1 Corinthians xv. 17.

The relation of the resurrection of Jesus to his atoning work is given by most commentators substantially as follows : The Christian is justified by the death of Christ who bore the penalty of his sins ; but faith on the part of the Christian is needed to make this justification effective, and for faith is needed knowledge. It is through the resurrection of Christ that the nature of his death is made known. Thus he was "raised on account of our justification," and if he had not been raised, the Christian would be yet in his sins.[1] Thus the resurrection is regarded as merely declarative.

It seems to me that Paul must have meant something more than this, or something different from it. It does not seem to me that he would have written to the Corinthians just what he did, if this had been what he meant. He says to them that if Christ be not risen their faith is vain, and they are yet in their sins. Their faith in what would be vain ? Certainly, if Christ was not raised, their faith in his resurrection would be vain. Paul must have meant more than this. He must have meant that their faith *in Jesus* would be vain if he had not risen. If they be-

[1] See, for instance, Meyer on the passages just quoted.

lieved that Christ had been raised when actually he had not, Christ could not have done something that they believed him to have done ; and this lacking something was essential to the work that they believed him to have accomplished. According to the interpretation generally received, they believed that Christ died in order that he might bear the penalty of the world's sin ; and his resurrection had conveyed to them the information that his death had this significance. If he had not been really raised, it is urged they had no basis for this belief.

The words seem to me to mean more than this. They seem to me to point to something essentially connected with the work of Christ itself. They imply not merely that if Christ were not raised the assurance of the Christian's faith would be gone, and that the matter would be left doubtful ; they make an absolute assertion that this faith would be vain if Christ had not been raised, and that his followers would be yet in their sins. It is an affirmation, not of the uncertainty of a hope, but of the certainty of its failure.

A more serious difficulty with the interpretation that makes the resurrection, in Paul's view, important because it declares that Christ in his death bore the penalty of the world's sin, lies in the fact that it does not declare this. I have studied the commentaries in vain to find any hint of the manner in which the resurrection of Christ declared his death to have had the substitutionary value that is claimed for it. With the best efforts on my own part, I find it impossible to conceive any way in which it could have had this significance. If the resurrection of Christ had any declarative force, it must have declared something with which it stood in the closest logical connection. It stands in no such logical relation with the idea that in his death he bore the world's sin.

Another attempt to reconcile the words of Paul with the traditional theory is made by Menegoz, who is quoted with approval by Pfleiderer,[1] though in a manner to leave it doubtful, to my own mind at least, whether Pfleiderer fully accepts the view or not. According to this view, Christ was condemned to death for our sins and was executed. By this execution he was set right with justice; thus he could not remain in death; he must be given back to life; therefore hath God raised him. As it is the right of the

[1] *Paulinismus* (second edition), p. 160.

thief condemned to prison to come back into freedom after suffering his penalty, so it was the right of Christ, after dying for the atonement of our sins, to return to life when this atonement had been accomplished. This theory is interesting as a protest against the traditional view, and gives a certain significance to the fact of the resurrection. We see that if Christ had died in order that he might bear the penalty of the world's sin, it is possible that he might have arisen when this result had been achieved. On the other hand, there would have been no particular reason to expect this.

If Jesus died in man's stead and thus satisfied the law, he and the men whose penalty he had paid stood on the same footing before the law. What further would have taken place, I, for one, have not the ingenuity to conjecture. So much at least appears clear, however, namely, that there was no more reason to expect him to arise at once from the dead than to expect those for whom he died to arise. They were by him set right with the law, and their immediate resurrection was to be expected at least as truly as his. Even then, if we grant all that is urged by Menegoz, it shows only that Christ might have arisen, not that he must have arisen. It furnishes no explanation of Paul's words to the Corinthians, that if Christ were not risen they were yet in their sins. It was something that followed the completion of the atoning work of Christ. It was not, as Paul insists, a part of this atoning work. In a word, the theory of Menegoz seems to me an artificial addition to an artificial theory. It is like an epicycle vainly used to supplement the inadequate cycle.[1]

I thus fail to find any method by which the resurrection of Christ may be made to appear to have any vital relation to his atoning work, as this work is commonly understood. We have now to ask whether the general interpretation of the teaching of Paul which I am here presenting will throw any better light upon the importance which he attached to the resurrection of Christ. In approaching this theme, we find ourselves at a disadvantage from which we have thus far been free. By starting from the most concrete and definite statements of Paul, and using these to explain the more vague and ab-

[1] I am sorry to have to refer to so important a work as that of Menegoz at second hand. When I tried to procure it, it was unfortunately out of print.

stract, we have been able to reach results which,
to me at least, seem well established, without
being obliged to call to our aid conjecture and
speculation. We have found explicit authority
for all the conclusions which have been reached.
So far as the subject before us is concerned, we
have no words of Paul or of his followers to guide
us. We know only that in the thought of Paul
the resurrection filled an important part in the
work of Christ, and was essentially connected
with his redemptive work.

Let us first assume, as the commentators for
the most part do, that the relation of the resurrection to the death of Christ is found in the fact
that it declared the nature and object of this;
and let us ask, What was the revelation which it
brought to Paul? In doing this, let us avoid all
conjecture; but starting with what we know to
have been in the mind of Paul, ask what effect
the resurrection must have had upon his thought.
We have indeed already anticipated this inquiry.[1]
Paul, as we have seen, persecuted the Christians
because he conceived that Christ was by the law
accursed, and that his followers shared his pollution. When Christ appeared in the glory of the

[1] See pp. 152 ff.

Father, Paul could not help seeing that, although accursed before the law, he was accepted and glorified by God. We have already seen how this could not help forcing the logical mind of Paul to leap to the conclusion that the condemnation of the Christian by the law had another side. If Jesus were thus raised and glorified, he must be the Christ of God. If he were the Christ, the fact that he was before the law accursed meant that for the Christian the reign of the law was over, and that the sins committed under the law disappeared with it. Here we have a revelation that is logically bound up with the events themselves.

Let us now take a step further and ask if the resurrection could have had, as to Paul it seems to have had, anything more than a declarative force. It is at this point that we are reduced to conjecture, and can only strive to make our conjectures keep within the limits of logical probability.

In Paul's doctrine the crucified Christ was under the curse of the law. The fact that he bore this curse would not have helped man, so at least we may conceive, unless Christ had triumphed over it. Without this triumph Christ and his followers would have remained accursed. The resurrection, however, changed the curse into victory. It was not merely that the spirit of Christ manifested itself in glory. It was not the spirit of Christ which was accursed. It was the body which was defiled and defiling. Unless this triumphed also, there would have been no redemption. It was the resurrection of the body that was thus the essential thing — its resurrection in glory. This was not merely declarative of a triumph ; it constituted the triumph. Such we may at least conceive to have been Paul's thought. We see how with this thought the resurrection may have been a direct and indispensable element in the justification, and how, if Christ had not risen, his followers would have been still in their sins.

I have spoken as if Paul's thought included the resurrection of the body of Christ. We find, indeed, in Paul's writings no indication of the crude conception which marks the story in the Gospels. Paul's notion of the resurrection in general must remain somewhat vague to us, as it very possibly was to him, so far as the relations between the earthly and the heavenly body are concerned. Perhaps this was to Paul among the

"Things which eye saw not, and ear heard not,
And which entered not into the heart of man."[1]

Two elements only are clear : one is that of identity ; the other is that of difference. What was raised was in some sense the same, and in some sense different from that which was sown. "Flesh and blood," he tells us, "cannot inherit the kingdom of God."[2] Yet there must have been some identity in which the earthly and heavenly states were united, or the term "resurrection" would have no significance. "So also," he tells us, "is the resurrection of the dead. It is sown in corruption ; it is raised in incorruption."[3] The "it," vague, yet precise, marks the element of identity, though it throws no light upon the manner in which the identity is preserved. Thus in the resurrection of Christ, that which was crucified and defiled was in some sense raised and glorified. Thus Christ endured the curse of the law and triumphed over it. He came forth as a conqueror ; "and opened the kingdom of heaven to all believers," to the Gentile no less than to the Jew.

There is one other passage in reference to the

[1] 1 Corinthians ii. 9.   [2] 1 Corinthians xv. 50.
[3] 1 Corinthians xv. 42.

resurrection of Christ which should be considered here. It is found in the Epistle to the Romans. This passage, in the Revised Version, reads : " Who was declared to be the Son of God, with power, according to the spirit of holiness, by the resurrection of the dead." [1] For the word "declared," which is retained from the Authorized Version, there is a substitute suggested in a note, namely, the word "determined." Unless the word " declared " is used in an un-English sense,[2] it certainly does not represent the meaning of the original. This use of the unsuitable or ambiguous word "declared " may perhaps illustrate the difficulty which is found in reconciling this passage with the generally received idea of Paul's teaching. In the passages which we have already considered, the resurrection has been by most treated as if it were merely declarative ; and in the one before us the word " declared" stands in the translation itself in spite of the unquestionable meaning of the Greek. This, perhaps, may be regarded as a confession of the weakness of the prevailing interpretation of Paul's teaching.

[1] Romans i. 4.

[2] That is, in the sense of the French *nommer.*

The passage is, indeed, looked at superficially, a singular one. In the third verse Christ is distinctly spoken of as "the Son of God," and yet in the fourth verse, in the course of the same sentence, he is said to be " determined to be the Son of God by the resurrection of the dead." The question naturally presses, How could he be determined to be that which he already was ? Pfleiderer, in the first edition of his " Paulinismus," emphasizes this difficulty, and thinks that he finds a contradiction in the thought of Paul, who had not fully wrought out in his mind the different elements which entered into his idea of the nature of Jesus. He says : " The historical and the ideal elements are joined, indeed, for the first time in the Christology of Paul, but as yet so little wrought out that their want of cohesion is everywhere apparent." [1]   In the later edition of the same work the passage is passed over more lightly.   In the earlier edition of Meyer's Commentary, the declarative interpretation has some place.   In the later edition the term " instituted " is used.[2]   No further expla-

[1] English translation, i. 159.   In this discussion Pfleiderer insists upon the proper meaning of the word.

[2] In the English translation.

nation of the passage is suggested by Meyer.
Whether the idea is, or is not, that of a formal
inauguration, so to speak, we are not told.   Further, it is not clear how, if Christ had been from
eternity the Son of God in the glory of the Father,
the resurrection, which was simply a return to
his original place, could be regarded as an institution or an inauguration, still less as an absolute constitution.   Clearly the resurrection filled
a place in the thought of Paul which it does not
fill in the thought of his later interpreters. This
later thought can see in it nothing more than
a declaration or a manifestation, with whatever
phrases this thought may be beclouded.

The interpretation which we have been following shows at least, as other interpretations do
not, what profound relation the resurrection of
Jesus *may have had* to his redemptive work.   If
we assume our conjectural explanation of the
place which, according to the idea of Paul, the
resurrection filled in the general scheme of redemption ; and if we further assume that the
words " the Son of God " here stand in a certain
more or less technical sense for the Messiah, the
passage has an easy and natural meaning. Christ
is first introduced as the Son of God ; he is then

said to have been born of the seed of David according to the flesh, — these last words marking
the antithesis between his earthly birth and his
previously recognized sonship to God. Then he
is said to have been determined to be the Son of
God with power by the resurrection of the dead.
If our conjecture is correct, it was by the resurrection that, in the thought of Paul, Christ became
indeed the Messiah. In it the work of atonement and of justification was accomplished. By
it the law was annulled ; and thus through it the
remission of sins was accomplished, and there
was open to the Christian the life of faith and of
liberty and of sonship to God.

Other New Testament Writings.

It may be interesting to glance at the epistles
that were written by, or that bear the names of,
other apostles, and notice the relation in which
these stand to the Pauline ideas.

Wonder has often been expressed at the fact
that the epistle that bears the name of James
makes no reference to the atoning death of
Christ. I have no need to enter into the discussion of the authorship of this epistle. Weizsäcker, who denies that it is by James, affirms

it to be of Jewish-Christian origin.[1]   It is then,
we may assume, written either by James or by a
follower of his.   This being so, the omission of
any reference to the atoning death of Christ is
precisely what we should expect, if the view of
Paul's teaching that I have been urging be correct.   James, as tradition tells us, remained loyal
to the Jewish law, and frequented diligently the
temple.   The words of the epistle that bears his
name are in keeping with this.   Apparently in
opposition to the exultant claim of Paul and his
followers that they had found liberty by the abolition of the law, the writer of this epistle speaks
of the law as a " law of liberty."   He speaks of
" looking into the perfect law, the law of liberty." [2]   The reference of this passage to the
Jewish law appears to me to be the only interpretation consistent with the generally accepted
Jewish-Christian origin of this epistle.   It is as
if, in opposition to the Anarchists who seek for
liberty by the destruction of the law, we should
to-day claim to find liberty in and through the
law.   If we understand the expression to refer
not to the Jewish law, but to the liberty that
is in Christ, the presence of this Pauline catch-

[1] *Das Apostolische Zeitalter*, p. 365.   [2] James i. 25.

word must show either that the epistle was not written by James or by any other Jewish Christian; or else that if James wrote it, he had become converted to the Pauline doctrine, which would be contradictory to a recognized tradition.

As we have seen, the teaching of Paul was that the remission of sins was the secondary, not the primary, result of the crucifixion of Christ. The primary result of this was the abolition of the law, so far as the Christian was concerned. The law having been abolished, the offences against the law were passed over, for the Christian had become free from its condemnation. Thus, to those who remained loyal to the law, the death of Christ had not the atoning efficacy which it had for Paul and his followers.

The Jewish Christian might believe that he was forgiven and saved through his faith in Christ. This result was, however, accomplished; because by faith in Christ he had become a member of the Messianic kingdom, and because, as the epistle before us insists, this faith took form in righteous deeds. For him, however, there could be no atoning death. Thus the silence of James, or of whatever Jewish Christian was the author of this epistle, is precisely what we should expect.

Weizsäcker, indeed, maintains that the doctrine of the remission of sins by the death of Christ was part of the primitive belief of the Christian church.[1] For this view he appeals to the words of Paul : " For I delivered unto you first of all that which also I received, how that Christ died for our sins according to the scripture." [2] He assumes that when Paul says he " received " this, his meaning was that he received it from the apostolic church. Meyer and Schmiedel take also a similar view of the passage. This view, which makes Paul refer his teaching to the authority of the apostolic church, appears to me to contradict his ordinary manner of speech. Of his gospel, he says : " For I make known to you, brethren, as touching the gospel which was preached by me, that it is not after man. For neither did I receive it from man, nor was I taught it, but it came to me through revelation of Jesus Christ. . . . But when it was the good pleasure of God, who separated me, even from my mother's womb, and called me through his grace, to reveal his Son in me, that I might preach him among the Gentiles ; immediately I

[1] *Das Apostolische Zeitalter* (second edition), p. 108.

[2] 1 Corinthians xv. 3.

conferred not with flesh and blood : neither went I up to Jerusalem to them which were apostles before me : but I went away into Arabia; and again I returned unto Damascus." [1] Paul goes on to tell of a visit that he made to Jerusalem after three years, and how little he there saw of the apostles. When Paul thus disclaims all human authority for his teaching, there seems an antecedent improbability that he should elsewhere say that he had received from man so important an element of his teaching as the doctrine of the remission of sins. At least, we should expect that if he so far deviated from his custom as to state this, he would feel the need of making perfectly clear what he meant. In a matter of interpretation, however, we have to ask primarily, not what we should expect, but what the writer actually said.

In regard to the passage before us (1 Corinthians xv. 3) Weizsäcker and Schmiedel content themselves with saying that Paul must have meant that he received from the earlier disciples the doctrine that Christ died for the remission of sins, because he does not say that he received it from the Lord. Meyer adds two other

[1] Galatians i. 11–17.

reasons.   One of these he derives from the fact
that the passage goes on to speak of merely historical incidents for which no revelation would
be needed.   We must, however, notice that only
a little earlier in the same epistle Paul had spoken
of his knowledge of the last supper as having
been given him by revelation.   He wrote: "For
I received of the Lord that which also I delivered
unto you, how that the Lord Jesus in the night
in which he was betrayed took bread;"[1] and
he proceeds to relate the story of the touching
transaction.   Now if Paul, in the eleventh chapter, speaks of having "received" his knowledge
of this historical incident from the Lord, it is idle
to insist that what, in the fifteenth chapter of
the same epistle, he speaks of having "received"
could not have been from the Lord because of
the historic facts involved.

Meyer further argues that the "received"
must refer to man, because it is correlated with
"deliver": "For I delivered unto you first of
all that which also I received."   The argument
would seem to be, that since the doctrine was
delivered to the Corinthians by a man, — namely,
Paul, — this man must also have received it from

[1] 1 Corinthians xi. 23 ff.

men. We must notice, however, that in the passage just quoted from the eleventh chapter in regard to the Lord's Supper, there is precisely the same correlation of the same words : " For I received of the Lord that which also I delivered unto you." The words in the original are the same in both cases, — παρέλαβον and παρέδωκα.

My criticism of Meyer's reasoning might seem at first sight not to bear with its full force against him. He insists that the preposition used by Paul in the statement in the fifteenth chapter (ἀπὸ) might signify an indirect communication from the Lord, and not a direct revelation. This, however, does not really affect my argument, as, whether the communication was direct or indirect, it was still from the Lord, and not by tradition from the brethren. It should be said, also, that his American editor, Dr. Chambers, makes light of Meyer's suggestions as to the preposition ἀπὸ. Thus what I have urged against Meyer's argument would hold good without qualification to all who do not accept his somewhat strained construction of the preposition in the earlier passage. Meyer's interpretation of both these passages would seem to show a desire to avoid the idea that Paul received a knowledge of generally known historic facts by revelation from the Lord, which desire led him to force unduly (according to Dr. Chambers) the meaning of the preposition used by Paul in the eleventh chapter, and to fail to recognize the importance of this passage in the examination of the corresponding expression in the fifteenth chapter.

There remains the argument used by all three of the authorities cited, namely, that "received" cannot refer to the Lord, because the Lord is not mentioned. In regard to this, the common-sense view would seem to be, that after having once spoken of his knowledge of the life of Jesus as having been received by revelation, Paul did not think it necessary to complete the formula every time it was used, but took it for granted that it would be completed in the minds of his readers ; and doubtless the simple-minded Corinthians did so understand the matter. Certainly, the commentators before Meyer did not doubt that Paul meant that he "received" his knowledge from the Lord.[1]

It appears to me that the critics confound an assumption that would be natural in general

[1] Cf. Meyer, a. l.

with a presumption that is natural in a special case. If, for instance, a man should say to us that he had heard of such or such an occurrence in some distant spot, we should assume that he had gathered it from public prints or common rumor. But suppose we know that the person who tells the story has a correspondent in the place referred to, and that he has been in the habit of quoting from this friend's letters, saying: " I have heard this or that from my friend at," wherever the scene of the event might be. In this case, when he said, " I have heard that such a thing has taken place," we should assume that he had received it from private correspondence unless he said otherwise. So at least it seems to me. At any rate, the probability against this is not strong enough to be the basis of an argument.

At the same time, if any insist that in the passage under consideration Paul must have meant that he " received " the information from the earlier disciples, I would suggest that, as he is going on to speak of external facts of Christ's history, all leading up to the various reappearances after his resurrection, it is possible that, naming his death, he added the explanatory " for

our sins " out of his own accustomed manner of
speech.   My own view, however, is that the correspondence between this passage and that in
the eleventh chapter of the same epistle (23–25),
to which reference has been made, is so great
that it is a rationalistic forcing of it to explain
it differently.

The " Epistle of James " gives such an interesting insight into the Christianity of that part
of the early church which did not accept Paul's
teaching, that it has seemed to me worth while
to dwell a little upon an interpretation of Paul's
words that, as it seems to me, confuses the whole
picture of the primitive-church.   I conceive that
the " Epistle of James " does not refer to the
atoning death of Christ, simply because for James
and his followers there was no such atoning
death ; and that Paul did not receive his doctrine
of the remission of sins by the death of Christ
from the apostles into whose fellowship he entered, because till he taught it that doctrine was
not known.

In regard to Paul's claim that his doctrine of
the remission of sins by the death of Christ was
received from the Lord, we may take either of
two views.   We may assume that when Christ

appeared to Paul, or when Paul believed that
Christ appeared to him, the vision imparted to
him the doctrine which he afterward preached;
or, without judging anything in regard to the
nature of this vision, we may assume that when
Paul saw, or believed that he saw, the crucified
one appearing in the divine glory, the whole logical result of the situation flashed at once through
his mind. If the crucified one was glorified,
then he had triumphed over the curse which the
law had uttered. Christ and his church then
stood outside of the law and were free from it;
and thus the old scores which had been accumu-
lating under the law were wiped out. It is con-
ceivable that this insight came in a moment, and
was thus so bound up with the vision that it became a part of it to his memory, and seemed to
him like a sudden revelation. Of course, this
explanation would not apply with equal force to
those matters of historical detail that Paul
claimed to have received by revelation. I recognize and feel all the difficulties involved in regard to these. It is a difficulty, however, that
we have to face in the one case (1 Corinthians
xi. 23); there is, therefore, no reason why we
should not face it in the other.

Turning now to the "First Epistle of Peter," we find language which is precisely similar to that used by Paul. Thus we read : "Knowing that ye were redeemed, not with corruptible things, with silver or gold, from your vain manner of life handed down from your fathers ; but with precious blood, as of a lamb without blemish and without spot, even the blood of Christ."[1] The epistle from which this extract is taken is addressed "to the elect who are of the sojourners of the dispersion."[2] The "vain manner of life handed down from your fathers" can be nothing other than the life according to the Mosaic law, with the traditions that had grown up about it. In saying to his readers that they were freed by the blood of Christ from their vain manner of life handed down from the fathers, the writer meant just what the writer to the Hebrews meant when he spoke of the blood of Christ as cleansing the consciences of his followers from dead works.[3] After this Pauline utterance, we can have no hesitation in explaining in the Pauline sense the passage in the second chapter : "Who his own self bare our sins in his body upon the tree."[4]

[1] I Peter i. 18 f.

[2] I Peter i. I.

[3] Hebrews ix. 14.

[4] I Peter ii. 24.

The writer of the epistle was evidently thoroughly converted to the Pauline doctrine. If the author were Peter himself, this Paulinism need not surprise us. That Peter had accepted Paul's doctrine is evident from Paul's language in his letter to the Galatians, though it would also appear that he was at that time a timid follower. Paul writes of him : " For before that certain came from James, he did eat with the Gentiles : but when they came, he drew back and separated himself, fearing them that were of the circumcision. And the rest of the Jews dissembled likewise with him ; insomuch that even Barnabas was carried away with their dissimulation."[1] If Peter had not believed it right to eat with the Gentiles, he would not have done so. When certain from James came there was a stampede among the disciples of Paul, including even so true a follower as Barnabas, not because their views had changed, but because they wished to stand well with the delegates from Jerusalem. Indeed, so far as the freer life was concerned, the teaching of Paul was ordinarily not, " You must not," but " You need not." Paul says of himself : " To the Jews I became as a Jew."[2]

[1] Galatians ii. 12 f.   [2] 1 Corinthians ix. 20.

Thus the temporary defection of Peter indicates no permanent opposition. It would seem to have been the result of a momentary impulse of cowardice, like that which led him to deny his Master, and to have had no greater significance.

If the " First Epistle of Peter " was not by the apostle but by a later hand, written after the Pauline doctrine had obtained wide recognition, it is not strange that it should utter this doctrine.

We cannot conclude this part of our discussion without noticing the phraseology that, in the account of the institution of the last supper as given in the Gospel according to Matthew, Jesus is represented as using. Jesus, it is there said, "took a cup and gave thanks, and gave to them, saying, Drink ye all of it ; for this is my blood of the covenant, which is shed for many unto remission of sins."[1] The closing words of this saying would appear to be wholly opposed to the view that I have been urging. I have assumed, as a result of the previous argument, that the idea of remission of sins by the blood of Christ was not held before, or outside of, the Pauline teaching. If Jesus before his

[1] Matthew xxvi. 27, 28.

death said that his blood was shed for the remission of sins, it would imply that this was one of
the earliest and most generally accepted doctrines of the apostolic church. It is to be noticed, however, that this phrase occurs in no
other account of the transaction. This suggests
the idea that it was an expression that naturally
crept into the version of the story, when the
thought of the blood of Christ had become completely united with the thought of the remission
of sins, which was believed to be accomplished
by it. I dislike to adopt the method that I am
in the habit of calling the *exegesis ignaviæ*, in
order to get a troublesome passage out of the
way. I therefore gladly quote the decision of
Meyer, which is based wholly on general principles, as he held no view of the matter that could
affect his judgment. He says : " It is to be
observed, further, that the genuineness of the
words εἰς ἄφεσιν ἁμαρτιῶν is put beyond all suspi-
cion by the unexceptionable evidence in their
favor (in opposition to David Schultz), although,
from their being omitted in every other record
of the institution of the supper, they should not
be regarded as having been originally spoken
by Christ, but as an explanatory addition, intro-

duced into the tradition and put into the mouth of Christ."

No book of the New Testament uses more intense sacrificial language in regard to the death of Christ than The Revelation of Saint John. We read of those " who have washed their robes, and made them white in the blood of the Lamb." [1]   Christ is spoken of as the " Lamb that was slain ; " [2] even as " the Lamb that hath been slain from the foundation of the world." [3] Nothing but the picturesque intensity of these expressions distinguishes them from phrases that are familiar in the Pauline literature. If, indeed, the assumption of Baur were to be accepted, and we were to consider the Apocalypse as an anti-Pauline document, then the use of such forms of speech would be of great importance, so far as the views that I am urging are concerned. I have maintained that the sacrificial terms used in regard to the death of Christ received their significance from the fact that Jesus, by the pollution of his crucifixion, made his followers outcast from the Jewish sanctities, and thus free of any allegiance to them ; and that with the

[1] Revelation vii. 14.   [2] *Ibid*. v. 12, *et passim*.
[3] *Ibid*. xiii. 8.

law disappeared the condemnation of the sins that had been committed against it. I have further assumed that outside of the Pauline Christianity such sacrificial language would have neither significance nor use. If The Revelation is a thoroughly anti-Pauline work, this latter part of my theory would have to be given up. The former part of it fits so perfectly the language of Paul and his school that, as it seems to me, it could not be disturbed. Baur's view finds, however, little recognition at present.

Weizsäcker presents a view intermediate between that of Baur and the one more generally held at present. He admits that the book does not represent the narrowness of the early Jewish Christians. It does not demand obedience to the law. It does not insist upon circumcision. He insists, however, that the writer has reached this result in his own way, and not by that of Paul. He claims that there is in the book no trace of Paul's thought.[1]

The idea urged by Weizsäcker, that the same result was reached by two different processes, appears to me not to conform to the probabilities of history. The law of parsimony may be

[1] Weizsäcker, *Das Apostolische Zeitalter* (second edition), p. 507.

used in reference to historical movements as well as to the processes of nature. At least it appears to me that it would apply to a case like that before us. There would seem but two ways in which freedom from the law could be reached : one is the strictly legal method followed by Paul ; the other is the more or less gradual discarding of what has come to appear superfluous. This latter naturally requires time, and would be delayed by the partisan spirit which the course of Paul roused in the early Jewish Christian. Such considerations, however, I admit are of little value, especially in a case like the present, where we have the facts before us. The question is, then, whether the fundamental thought of the Apocalypse is, or is not, in harmony with that of Paul.

We notice, in the first place, that the whole framework of the book, the forms of the thought, and the method of presentation, are wholly unlike anything in the Pauline literature. It is evidently written by a patriotic Jew. Jerusalem is still to the author the type of the heavenly city, even though the earthly Jerusalem be accursed.[1] So marked is this Jewish character

[1] Revelation xi. 8.

that it lends a certain antecedent probability
to the theory of Vischer, that the basis of the
work is a Jewish apocalyptic writing which has
been adapted more or less rudely to Christian
use. The very preponderance of this Jewish
element makes all the more marked the freedom
of the book from any Judaizing tendency. The
form, then, is even less Pauline than that of the
Epistle to the Hebrews.

When we look at the substance of the thought
the result is different. We find no Pauline
phraseology, but we do find the Pauline idea.
While there is nothing about "salvation by
faith," there is recognized the fact that the
robes of the saints have been washed and made
white in the blood of the Lamb. The saints
have been accepted through the sacrifice of
Christ. How could the death of Christ have
been made available to them? By no conceiva-
ble way except by faith. The Pauline word is
not there, but the Pauline thought is implied.
On the other hand, the book lays great stress
upon righteousness. Not by faith but by works
are men to be saved. This, however, can stand
in no contradiction with the idea of salvation by
the blood of Christ, which, as we have seen, is

so prominent in the book. Here, also, the difference from the Pauline manner of speech is one of emphasis. Paul teaches salvation by faith ; he teaches freedom from the law ; at the same time he urges that "if any man hath not the Spirit of Christ, he is none of his." [1] If the writer of The Revelation cries, "Without are the dogs, and the sorcerers, and the fornicators, and the murderers, and the idolaters, and every one that loveth and maketh a lie:" [2] Paul exclaimed, "Know ye not that the unrighteous shall not enter the kingdom of God." [3] If we thus find the Pauline thought, there is no reason to doubt that it was reached by the Pauline way.

Freedom from the law and forgiveness were, according to The Revelation, as according to Paul, reached through the death of Christ. Christ here, as with Paul, was set forth to be a propitiation for sins. Paul gives a distinct and logical argument to prove that the death of Christ must have produced this effect. He shows us precisely in what manner the crucifixion produced this effect. The writer of the Apocalypse assumes that the death of Christ

---

[1] Romans viii. 9.   [2] Revelation xxii. 15.

[3] 1 Corinthians vi. 9.

had this propitiatory effect, but he gives no hint as to how the death of Christ operated to this end. The signification attached to sacrifices in the ancient world shows that this sacrificial language as applied to the death of Christ cannot mean that he bore vicariously the penalty of men's sins. The sacrificial language would suggest no such idea. There seems, then, no reason to consider the relation of the believer to Christ as it is presented in the Apocalypse to be fundamentally different from that which is presented by Paul.

Weizsäcker makes the writer of The Revelation give a somewhat grudging welcome to the uncircumcised Christian. Where it is said, " After these things I saw, and behold, a great multitude, which no man could number, out of every nation, and of all tribes and peoples and tongues, standing before the throne and before the Lamb, arrayed in white robes, and palms in their hands ; " and the explanation is given, " These are they which come out of the great tribulation, and they washed their robes, and made them white in the blood of the Lamb." [1] Weizsäcker intimates that these heathen confessors are ac-

[1] Revelation vii. 9 and 14.

cepted because, through the great tribulation, they have obtained a share in the martyrdom of the Lamb.[1] This idea is read into the passage and not gathered from it. The reasoning might as well have been to the effect that even these martyrs, if martyrs they were, could be accepted only through the death of Christ. They were those who had come out of the great tribulation. If, as it would appear, this great tribulation was that which was to be connected with the grand consummation so speedily to be accomplished, the expression may perhaps stand for the redeemed in general.

[1] Weizsäcker, *Das Apostolische Zeitalter* (second edition), p. 506.

CHAPTER V.

PAUL'S PHILOSOPHY OF HISTORY.

BEFORE considering the positive side of Paul's teaching, it is important to glance at the view which he took of the general history of man. Paul had his Philosophy of History as truly as any of our later thinkers; and it is impossible to understand his idea of Christianity except as we see it in relation to his whole theory of life.

The Fall.

So far as his specific statements go, we must start with the notion of the Fall. "Through one man," he tells us, "sin entered into the world, and death through sin; and so death passed unto all men, for that all sinned;" or as it is otherwise translated, "for that all have sinned."[1] Here, then, begins the great movement of history. Obviously, this saying points back to a time when there was neither death nor sin. In

[1] Romans v. 12.

all this Paul is, to a large extent, uttering the
common thought of his time and people. In
what manner the posterity of Adam was affected
by the sin of their first parent, Paul does not tell
us. To the verse that I quoted I gave, so far
as the last clause is concerned, a duplicate rendering. Meyer, for instance, with whom the Revised Version agrees, insists upon the strict interpretation of the aorist, making the passage read,
"For that all sinned." Other interpreters, as
Lipsius, use the perfect form, "For that all have
sinned." The translation of the Vulgate is still
different. In that we read, "In whom all sinned."
Unquestionably this phrase did very much to
give form to the notion of the Fall as it has been
held by the Christian church. Such picturesque
translations or mistranslations have not unfre-
quently shaped the thought even of theologians.
The interpretation of Meyer and the Revised
Version would seem, however, to amount to very
much the same thing as the translation of the
Vulgate ; the force of the aorist, "For that all
sinned," putting the sinning at a definite moment, which would be that on which Adam
sinned. The other translation, "For that all
have sinned," would obviously detach the sin of

Adam's posterity to a certain extent from the sin of Adam. Each individual would be regarded as having sinned on his own account.[1] Into these niceties of Greek construction I will not enter. I will only remark that if we assume Weber to represent the Rabbinical teaching in regard to the relation of man's sin to the sin of Adam, the freer translation, "for that all have sinned," is more in conformity with the teachings of the later Jews. According to the Rabbinical teaching as presented by Weber, there is implanted in men no irresistible necessity of sinning; but there is in all men a tendency to sin so mighty that hardly any individual can resist it.[2]

Paul would thus seem to have gone beyond the teaching of his time, so far as the necessity of sinning is concerned. The Rabbinical teachers were possibly governed by the ethical presumption which the entire Hebrew history had done so much to strengthen. They may have wished to preserve some place, however slight, for human responsibility. They may have shrunk

[1] Dr. Dwight, the American editor of Meyer's *Commentary on the Romans*, insists that the aorist is used by Paul figuratively.

[2] Weber's *System der Palästinischen Theologie*, p. 231.

from the notion of a complete loss of the freedom which could alone make sin really sinful.
Perhaps for this reason they clung to this formal
recognition of the rights of the will in the presence of a tendency to sin which was practically
overmastering. On the other hand, it is possible
that Paul was unconsciously led by his enthusi-
asm for the work of Christ, and the deliverance
that came through him, to emphasize the absolute helplessness of man in the presence of the
sinful diathesis which he had inherited. From
Adam man had received a taint which made it
impossible for him to escape from the corruption
of sin. "They that are in the flesh," he tells us,
"cannot please God." [1] Paul's whole teaching
implies that this does not mean merely that
those who are living in conformity with the
flesh cannot please God. Until the taint is removed, no soul can help living in accordance
with the flesh. On the other hand, Paul does
not teach that the flesh originally contained an
element of sinfulness. His language is explicit.
"Through one man sin entered into the world." [2]

[1] Romans viii. 8.

[2] Romans v. 12. See Dickson's *Saint Paul's Use of the Terms
Flesh and Spirit*, chapter xi. ; especially p. 319.

It was not transgression that entered ; it was sin. It was not merely that sin showed itself for the first time in the disobedience of Adam. With this disobedience sin entered into the world. If sin at that time entered into the world, it could not have been already bound up with the flesh. Moreover, if the flesh were by its very constitution sinful, it would have been impossible for this sinfulness to have been removed by Christ. According to Paul's teaching, then, there was introduced into the flesh a quality of sinfulness which rendered it impossible for man to obtain righteousness and to please God.

The Promise to Abraham.

The second great step in the evolution of human history, according to the teaching of Paul, was the promise that was given to Abraham, " In thee shall all the nations be blessed." [1] Here begins a certain differentiation in the history of the world. Abraham was called of God. A promise was made to him and to his seed. His posterity was to be set apart from other men. They were to be a chosen people, the elect of God. They were to stand in a special relation

[1] Galatians iii. 8.

to God.   God was to be in a special manner their God.   They were to serve him, and he was to guide and protect them, and grant them his special favor.   This was, however, not on their own account or for their own special gain.   It was a process which was being carried on for the sake of the whole world.   The Hebrews were placed over against the world for the sake of the world. The course of human history was divided into two great lines of movement ; but this separation was with reference to a future reunion.   It was as when, for some strategic gain, an army is separated into two great divisions which are later to effect a junction.   Or we might, perhaps, say better, that the Hebrew people was like a division of an army detailed for some special purpose, which, when this purpose is accomplished, is to rejoin the main body.

In all this Paul took a view of the election of Israel very different from that held by his countrymen.   The Jews had felt themselves selected by God on account of his special favor.   The promises in regard to the coming Messiah they felt to be prophecies of their special glory. Through him they were to become the rulers of the world.   The nations were to be tributary to

Jerusalem. Paul shared with them the sense of the glory of his people ; but with him it was the glory of service. He interpreted the dignity of his race in the spirit of that saying of Jesus : " Whosoever would be first among you shall be your servant." [1] " What advantage then hath the Jew ? " he asks ; " or what is the profit of circumcision ? Much every way : first of all, that they were intrusted with the oracles of God." [2] The advantage of the Jew was thus that he was selected to be the bearer of the messages of God to men ; that he was to be the instrument in working out the great plan of salvation, the results of which were to be common to the race.

The Law.

The next stage in the unfolding of the plan of human history, as Paul understood it, was the giving of the law. It was that they might receive this law that the children of Abraham had been separated from the other nations of the earth. In this Paul agreed with the Jewish teachers. Indeed, he lagged not a whit behind the most patriotic and enthusiastic Jews in his estimate of the holiness and grandeur of the law. " The

[1] Matthew xx. 27.   [2] Romans iii. 1 f.

law," he tells us, "is holy, and the commandment
holy, and righteous, and good." [1]　And again he
cries : " For we know that the law is spiritual." [2]
When, however, he came to speak of the purpose
and the effect of the law, he differed absolutely
from the view of the Jews in general.　The view
which Paul held in regard to the calling of his
people was, as we have seen, different from that
held by them.　His view of the purpose for which
the law was given was diametrically opposite to
that of his people.　By this alone Paul would
have been utterly separated from the national
life.　The Jews believed that the law had been
given as a rule of conduct, and was designed to
lead men to righteousness.　It would have seemed
to them a truism to say that the law was given
in order that it might be obeyed.　It was one of
the most startling of the paradoxes in which the
thought of Paul took shape, that, according to
him, the law was given, not that it might be
obeyed, but that it might be disobeyed. [3]　The
law, he tells us, "was added because of trans-

1 Romans vii. 12.

2 Romans vii. 14.

3 Compare Pfleiderer's *Paulinismus* (second edition), p. 93,
and Meyer's *Commentary*, a. l.

gressions." [1]   More clearly rendered, the passage teaches that the law was added *for the sake
of* transgressions.   There were no transgressions, and there could have been none, before
the law was given.   In another place Paul says
with equal explicitness : "The law came in beside, that the trespass might abound." [2]   We
have then the starting proposition that the law
was set forth in order that it might be broken.

To understand this position, which seems at
first sight so strange, we must remember what
was, according to the teaching of Paul, the condition in which man was left by the sin of Adam.
As we have seen, by this sin the flesh received a
taint.   On the one side, man became mortal, so
that "death reigned from Adam until Moses,
even over them that had not sinned after the
likeness of Adam's transgression." [3]   During
this time there would seem to have been, according to the thought of Paul, no transgression, because there can be none without law ; and there
was no formal and express command of God from
the time Adam was forbidden to eat of the fruit
of the tree in the Garden of Eden until the time

[1] Galatians iii. 19.   [2] Romans v. 20.
[3] Romans v. 14.

when the law was given to Moses upon Sinai.
Paul, elsewhere, in the same epistle, speaks indeed of the law written upon the hearts of those
to whom the Mosaic law had not come ;[1] but
this he here leaves out of the account, regarding
it perhaps as of a less formal character. However this may be, whether there were or were
not transgressions, the taint of sin was there just
the same, and the result of this taint was death.

On the other hand, by this taint of sin men
were not only exposed to death, they were exposed to the wrath of God. "We . . . were by
nature," we read in the Epistle to the Ephesians,
"children of wrath, even as the rest;"[2] and in
the Epistle to the Romans we read: "They
that are in the flesh cannot please God."[3]

Sin was thus bound up in the very life of man.
It was like a disease which lurks in the system,
sapping its vitality, but of which the sufferer is
unconscious. The object of the law was to make
men conscious of their sinfulness. It was to
make them feel themselves helpless in the presence of this evil.

In this connection it is to be noticed that, not-

[1] Romans ii. 15.   [2] Ephesians ii. 3.
[3] Romans viii. 8.

withstanding all that he said of the power of sin, Paul did not teach the total depravity of man. There was an inner self, which was in a special manner *the* self, which was not corrupted by the sin of the flesh, but was held in bondage by it. " I delight," Paul said, " in the law of God after the inward man : but I see a different law in my members, warring against the law of my mind, and bringing me into captivity under the law of sin which is in my members." [1] It is interesting to notice how, in the whole passage from which these words are taken, Paul uses the pronouns " I " and " me," in reference to the higher life, thus identifying himself with it. It was precisely to stir up this double consciousness, the strife which this passage so eloquently describes, that the law was given.

Let us look more closely at the manner in which the law reaches this result. " The law came in," Paul tells us, " that the trespass might abound." [2]   Again he says : " For the law worketh wrath ; but where there is no law, neither is there transgression." [3]   " For when we were in the flesh, the sinful passions, which were through

[1] Romans vii. 22 f.   [2] Romans v. 20.

[3] Romans iv. 15.

the law, wrought in our members to bring forth fruit unto death." [1] " I had not known sin, except through the law : for I had not known coveting, except the law had said, Thou shalt not covet : but sin, finding occasion, wrought in me through the commandment all manner of coveting : for apart from the law sin is dead. And I was alive apart from the law once : but when the commandment came, sin revived, and I died ; and the commandment, which was unto life, this I found to be unto death : for sin, finding occasion, through the commandment beguiled me, and through it slew me. So that the law is holy, and the commandment holy, and righteous, and good. Did then that which is good become death unto me ? God forbid. But sin, that it might be shewn to be sin, by working death to me through that which is good ; — that through the commandment sin might become exceeding sinful." [2]

Quotations from Paul in regard to this matter need not be further multiplied. The last passage cited tells, however, the whole story. The object of the law was that sin might by it be made to appear exceeding sinful.

[1] Romans vii. 5.   [2] Romans vii. 7–14.

It must not be understood that sin was itself increased by the law. The law was not given for the sake of sin, but "for the sake of transgressions." The sin was there. It was a constant element of the life. I am not sure that it was not a fixed quantity. Through transgressions this latent sin manifested itself in all its ugliness.

The law was given for a double purpose. In the first place, its effect was to stir up sin, as one might stir up to rage a wild beast in the jungle, in order that one might do battle with it. In the second place, its effect was to make sin "appear exceeding sinful." It did this by the manifestation of the ideal holiness. Seeing this, men could feel as they had not felt before the sinfulness of their nature, by which they were separated from this ideal. Thus on the one side the soul was made to feel the reality and the hatefulness of sin ; on the other, it was made to realize and aspire towards the beauty of the divine ideal. Thus the law aroused both elements of the nature. It stimulated them to conflict. The inward man, we must assume, would not by itself have reached the conception of righteousness without the law any more than sin would without it have revealed its true nature. "I am carnal, sold under sin," said Paul; "for that which I do I know not: for not what I would, that do I practise; but what I hate, that I do. But if what I would not, that I do, I consent unto the law that it is good. So now it is no more I that do it, but sin which dwelleth in me. . . . I find then the law, that, to me who would do good, evil is present. For I delight in the law of God after the inward man: but I see a different law in my members, warring against the law of my mind, and bringing me into captivity under the law of sin which is in my members."[1] Throughout Paul identifies himself, as we have seen, with the side of righteousness. The sin is not his sin; it is in his members, that is, in his flesh. None the less he cannot escape from it. He feels himself in bondage to a power which is in him, but not of him. He cries: "O wretched man that I am! who shall deliver me out of the body of this death?"[2] When this exclamation has been uttered the law has done its work. It has brought the two elements of the nature each into the full consciousness of itself and of its opposite. The law has aroused sin to show

[1] Romans vii. 14–23.   [2] Romans vii. 24.

itself in its sinfulness. It has stimulated the inner man to assert itself. This inner man has seen and recognized the ideal of holiness. It feels itself in accord with this. It gives to it its whole reverence, and would give to it its whole obedience. The lower nature, however, holds it back. It is a struggle of life with death, — with death, the whole horror and loathsomeness of which it feels. All this the law has accomplished. It was what it was set to accomplish. It has done its work and may pass away.

One other aspect of the work of the law is alluded to by Paul, so far as I remember, only once, and then very briefly and somewhat vaguely. He writes to the Galatians : " But before faith came, we were kept in ward under the law, shut up unto the faith which should afterwards be revealed. So that the law hath been our tutor to bring us unto Christ." [1] Here Paul would seem to refer to the law as that which held the Jewish people together, giving them a distinctive unity, so that, amid all the changes that were going on around them, they should remain a chosen people, ready to receive the gospel when it came.

[1] Galatians iii. 23, 24.

The Transitoriness of the Law.

The next point that we have to recognize in Paul's scheme of history is his assumption that the law was from the beginning intended to be temporary. It was not an expedient that was tried and failed, and therefore gave place to something better. It was established to do a definite work, and with the intention that it should disappear when this work was accomplished. The law thus was, and was intended to be, self-limiting. The proof of this Paul found in the fact that the promise was given before the law was established. "To Abraham," he tells us, "his faith was reckoned for righteousness. How then was it reckoned? when he was in circumcision, or in uncircumcision? Not in circumcision, but in uncircumcision. . . . For not through the law was the promise to Abraham or to his seed, that he should be the heir of the world, but through the righteousness of faith. For if they which are of the law be heirs, faith is made void, and the promise is made of none effect." [1]

In the Epistle to the Galatians Paul uses language which is even more explicit. "And the

[1] Romans iv. 9–14.

scripture," he says, "foreseeing that God would justify the Gentiles by faith, preached the gospel beforehand unto Abraham, saying, In thee shall all the nations be blessed." [1] Here we have the distinct affirmation that it was foreseen that the Gentiles would be justified by faith; that is, that the law would at some time give way, that the wall which was set up in the law would be torn down, and that the Gentiles who had not known the law should become partakers of the promise.

It has become the custom to exaggerate the difference between the views of Paul and those of the writer to the Hebrews. In point of fact, both say substantially the same thing. It is very interesting to notice the freedom with which the writer to the Hebrews uses the ideas which he must have received from Paul. He does not repeat them as a learner might repeat his lesson. He shows that he has thoroughly appropriated them. He expresses them as freely as if they were of his own devising. The exposition is so independent that, looked at superficially, it seems to be treating of a wholly different matter. It is only when we reach the central thought of

[1] Galatians iii. 8.

each, that we find that their thoughts are the same. This shows how natural the thought of Paul was ; how it sprang of itself out of the circumstances of the time. Paul had simply to point, and men saw for themselves. We have already found in the last chapter of the Epistle to the Hebrews a most vivid presentation of Paul's view of the crucifixion, in which the form is entirely different from any which Paul himself had used. In the aspect of the case which we are here considering, the writer to the Hebrews reaches the same result at which Paul had arrived, but he illustrates it in a different manner. Where Paul spoke of Abraham, the writer to the Hebrews speaks of Melchizedek.[1] I am not sure that the latter example does not furnish the best illustration of the truth that both were striving to establish. This truth was, that the law, from its very inception, was intended to be exhibited as something limited and transient. In the Old Testament it is related that Abraham paid tithes to Melchizedek and received a blessing from him. This shows that Melchizedek must have been a greater personage than Abraham. In the homage which Abraham paid to

[1] Hebrews vi. and vii.

Melchizedek the descendants of Abraham were involved. In him the whole Levitical priesthood did reverence to this personage as to their superior. Paul had shown that the promise was given to Abraham before the establishment of the law. Around the narrow circle of the law he had drawn the larger circle of the life of Abraham. The writer to the Hebrews draws about the life of Abraham the still larger circle of that extra-Abrahamic life which was represented by Melchizedek. By this process the Mosaic law is exhibited in its real relation to the history of the world. It is as when we look down upon some city which had absorbed our life from some lofty height which reveals its insignificance. The patriarch Abraham stands in relations vaster than those of the law, while he himself bows before a still larger life.

The point which the writer to the Hebrews is urging becomes vastly more clear and important by his use of a verse of the one hundred and tenth Psalm upon which he seized with the insight of genius. We can only wonder that it escaped the vision of his great master Paul, and are forced to admire all the more the dialectic skill of this strangely unknown writer whose

words we are considering. The passage is this :
" The Lord hath sworn, and will not repent,
thou art a priest forever after the order of Melchizedek.[1] This verse was understood to refer
to the Messiah, and what important aspects of
his work does it suggest ! A priest after the
order of Melchizedek ! Of what order was the
priesthood of Melchizedek ? One thing is evident, namely, that it was not of the Levitical
order. If we should interpret the passage from
our own point of view, that is, from the point of
view of the simple student of history, we should
say that the priesthood of Melchizedek was of
the patriarchal order. This is to say, that it was
of an order which was not separated from the
relations of ordinary life. The patriarch was not
a priest because he was set apart to that office,
and thus stood aloof from the ordinary relations
of the world. He was a priest on account of
these relationships. It was because he lived
among his descendants as their head and their
ruler, that he was fitted to be the utterer of their
prayers and the performer of their sacrificial
rites. If Christ was a priest after the order of
Melchizedek it was because he stood like him in

[1] Psalm cx. 4; Hebrews v. 6.

the open. It was because he was not hedged
about by priestly limitations and specific ordinances. It was because he stood among men as
their actual leader in spiritual things, because
his natural attitude towards men fitted him to
be their priest, and indeed forced this priesthood
upon him ; it was for this that he stood to them
in this sacred relation. In a word, the priesthood of Christ resembled that of Melchizedek in
being an extra-Levitical priesthood, based not
upon priestly descent, but upon the general fitness of things. This, I say, is the resemblance
which we should find between the priesthood of
Christ and that of Melchizedek, if we looked at
the thing from a purely natural and historical
point of view. Whatever of mystical or allegori-
cal significance the writer to the Hebrews may
have introduced into the story of Melchizedek,
considerations similar to those that have just
been adduced lay at the bottom of his reasoning.
The writer insists that Melchizedek was without
father, without mother, and without genealogy,
meaning by this, as all admit, that he was not of
priestly descent ; that as a priest he was, as the
Romans would say, *novus homo*. Thus Paul emphasizes the fact that the priesthood of Christ

was not after the order of Aaron : " For he of whom these things are said belongeth to another tribe, from which no man hath given attendance at the altar. For it is evident that our Lord hath sprung out of Judah ; as to which tribe Moses spake nothing concerning priests."[1] Again, Christ hath been made a priest, "not after the law of a carnal commandment, but after the power of an endless life." [2]

The point which I wish to emphasize in all this is that to Paul and to his followers the law carried from the very start the marks of limitation. The doing away with the law was no after-thought ; it was bound up with its very structure. Christ standing outside the law joined hands with Abraham, as Abraham stood before the law was given. Standing in the midst of the Gentiles, Christ joined hands with Melchizedek, the Gentile priest and ruler to whom Abraham, and through him the whole Levitical priesthood, bowed, and to whom they paid tithes. The law coming between them could not separate them. It was like a cloud floating in the heavens, destined to be lost in the measureless expanse.

The law, then, was established for a definite

[1] Hebrews vii. 13 f.   [2] Hebrews vii. 16.

purpose, namely, to fit men to receive the great salvation that was to come through Christ. When this salvation came, the law was to pass away. The promise which had been by the law shut up unto the Jews was to break through this limitation, and was to include the Gentile world in its gracious sweep. The Lord, "through whom are all things,"[1] was to leave his preëxistent glory.[2] He was to descend to earth and be made in fashion as a man. He was to be "born of a woman, born under the law, that he might redeem them which were under the law."[3] How this deliverance was to be accomplished we have seen. The law was to be honored even in its displacement. It was itself to speak the word that should give liberty to the followers of Jesus. Jesus was, by his crucifixion, to become subject to the curse of the law. He was to become in the view of the law polluted and polluting. Through this legal pollution his followers were to become outlawed, and through this outlawry they were to become free.

[1] I Corinthians viii. 6.   [2] 2 Corinthians viii. 9.
[3] Galatians iv. 4, 5.

The Doctrine of Election.

Here we may conceive certain grave questions to have occurred to Paul. The Jews were the chosen people. The promise of the coming Messiah had been made to them. They had been guided and preserved for this event. How could it happen that just when the fulfilment of the promise had been reached, when the Messiah had actually come, the people to whom he came and who had prepared the way for this coming should fail to recognize him, should reject him with scorn, should crucify him, and thus render him accursed ? Behind this question may have arisen another which was yet more momentous. Suppose that all this had not happened ; suppose that the Jews had recognized their Messiah as might have been expected ; suppose that instead of crucifying him they had met him with submission and honor, and had cried, " Blessed is he that cometh in the name of the Lord ; " in this case, how could the work of the Messiah have been accomplished ? In what way could the law have been annulled ? Christ born under the law would have lived and died under the law ; how, then, would the promise to the

Gentiles have been fulfilled? The Jews would have had their Messiah, and the Gentiles would have remained "without hope and without God in the world." Surely this was too momentous a matter to be left to chance. The hand that had led the chosen people thus far, the hand that had guided Abraham in his wanderings, that had guided the children of Israel in their long and eventful history, could not leave them at this decisive moment of their career. Here we meet one of the boldest — we might say one of the most audacious — movements in the Pauline strategy. Just as Isaac had been chosen to be one of the great leaders in the development of the Hebrew race and to be the medium through which the promise given to Abraham was passed on to future ages, while Ishmael was left in the outer world of unconsecrated life,[1] so in this supreme moment the divine oversight showed itself in the choice of the instruments by which the consummation was to be accomplished. As Abraham and his descendants were detailed for the special duty of leading up the history of the world to the moment when the Messiah should appear, so now that he had appeared, Jews were

---

[1] Galatians iv. 21 ff.

detailed to the various offices which the fulfilment of the Messiah's work required. A small
part were appointed to be believers, in order
that so far as the Jews were concerned the
transaction might not be without avail; for it
would be incredible that among the chosen people there should be none to be the recipients
of the new grace and the transmitters of it to
the Gentile world. On the other hand, a part
of the Jewish people, and, as it would appear,
the larger part, were detailed to reject him.
Without their rejection of him in the form that
I have so often described, the work of the Messiah could not have been accomplished. Without
this the Jewish Christian would have remained
under the dominion and the condemnation of
the law; while the Gentiles would have been
shut out from any share in the divine promises
and from any hope of salvation. Over and over
again, in the Epistle to the Romans, Paul explains to the Gentiles, to whom he was writing,
that the blindness and disobedience of the Jews
were the means of the salvation of the Gentile
world. "I say then," cried Paul, "Did they
stumble that they might fall? God forbid: but
by their fall salvation is come unto the Gen-

tiles." [1] Their falling, it would appear from this, was not an end in itself, but the means to an end which could not have been accomplished without it. Again, we are taught that "the casting away of them is the reconciling of the world." [2] "Their fall," Paul says, "is the riches of the world, and their loss the riches of the Gentiles." [3] To his Gentile readers, Paul said: "As touching the gospel, they are enemies for your sake." [4] The Gentile was represented as saying, "Branches were broken off, that I might be grafted in." [5] In a word, the Gentiles had obtained mercy by the disobedience of the Jews. [6]

This is the signification of the doctrine of election urged by Paul, so far at least as the great emphasis laid upon it in the Epistle to the Romans is concerned; and it is this which justifies the prominent place given to the doctrine of election in this epistle, in which Paul presents in its most complete and systematic form his philosophy of history. He shows that in the past God has chosen his workmen as he would,

[1] Romans xi. 11.

[2] Romans xi. 15.

[3] Romans xi. 12.

[4] Romans xi. 28.

[5] Romans xi. 19.

[6] Romans xi. 30.

and has assigned to each his task. To some he has appointed an honorable service. Others he has made for service that was dishonorable. Both were alike his instruments. "Hath not the potter," he exclaims, "a right over the clay, from the same lump to make one part a vessel unto honour, and another unto dishonour?"[1] It is to be noted, however, that both are vessels designed for a certain use. The potter does not make a vessel for dishonor merely that it may be dishonored. He makes it, because there is a certain purpose that only such a vessel can accomplish. So, according to Paul, God chooses his instruments and shapes them to his use. They are, however, instruments by means of which his great purposes can be accomplished.

It is to be noted that the three cases in which Paul chiefly recognizes the manifestation of this power of election and reprobation are the three great epochs in the evolution of the divine plan as manifested in the history of Israel. The first was the setting apart of Israel to be the special people of God, by the election of Isaac and the rejection of Ishmael; and later and more strikingly by the election of Jacob and the rejection

[1] Romans ix. 21.

of Esau, "as it is written, Jacob I loved, but Esau I hated."[1] The second was the hardening of the heart of Pharaoh, when Israel was called forth from the yoke of the Egyptians to become an independent nation.[2] What part the hardening of Pharaoh's heart, so that he refused to let the people go, was supposed to play in the transaction we are not told. Possibly it was to insure the complete severance of the Israelites from the Egyptians. The two peoples parted in hate, and the separate and independent existence of Israel was thus established. Possibly, however, Paul had no other distinct thought than that God hardened Pharaoh's heart in the furtherance of his designs. The third case was that in which the Christians became free from the Jewish law. In this case, it is obvious that without the hardening of the hearts of the Jews this result would not have been reached, and the religion of Jesus would not have entered upon its independent life. So we read, "God gave them a spirit of stupor, eyes that they should not see, and ears that they should not hear, unto this very day."[3]

[1] Romans ix. 13.   [2] Romans ix. 17.
[3] Romans xi. 8.

Paul evidently felt that this view of the sovereignty of God might seem to strike at the foundations of morality. If men are serving God while they appear to be disobeying him, how can they be blamed?   If by means of the rejection of Christ by the Jews God was fulfilling his wise purposes, is not this act which seemed so criminal taken out of the category of wrongdoing?   Must we not justify the evil deed? Must we not go even farther than this, and recognize the general principle that wrong is not wrong, if it be performed for a good end? Indeed, if the Christians claimed that the rejection and crucifixion of Christ by the Jews were simply the working out of God's righteous plan, might not the impression be easily produced that they took this view of human actions in general, and might they not be slanderously reported as saying, " Let us do evil, that good may come?" [1]   So at least I am inclined to understand the somewhat obscure passage with which the third chapter of the Epistle to the Romans opens ; assuming that the first person is used to give greater vividness to the statement.   To the ethical difficulties that he raises Paul gives no

[1] Romans iii. 8.

theoretical solution. He sees a divine destiny controlling the acts that seem most free, and causing those that seem most wrong : and to the question, " Is God unrighteous who visiteth with wrath ? " he can only answer, " God forbid : for then how shall God judge the world ? " while the rumor that he maintained that wrong might be done for the sake of the good that should result he could only stamp as a vile slander.

There is no passage in which one sees more clearly within the compass of so few lines the working of the mind of Paul, as it is struck by one consideration after another. In the previous chapter he had been painting the shortcomings and the sins of the Jews. Then he recognized the possibility that the patriotism of some reader might protest ; perhaps his own patriotism protested, against this dark picturing of the life of the nation ; and the question arose, " What advantage then hath the Jew ? " His patriotism urged in answer the great mission to which the Jewish people had been called, that of being the bearers of the oracles of God. Then came with fresh sadness the thought of the unbelief of his people ; how unworthy they had proved of the great trust. Then he remembered that even in this unbelief they had been the servants of God, fulfilling his great purpose, manifesting his right-eousness. On the other hand, he saw that this was no exculpation, and that they were sinners none the less. At the last, all that could be said was that, in spite of this sin of unbelief, they were no worse than other men. The passage that began, "What advantage then hath the Jew?" and went on to the proud answer, "Much every way," ends with the humbler question, "What then? are we in worse case than they?" After the "Much every way," Paul had gone on to say, "*First of all*, that they were intrusted with the oracles of God." This, it would seem, was to have been the first heading of a series of patriotic claims; but as Paul went on he was overpowered by the shame of the unbelief of his people, and by the thoughts that were suggested by this. He never got farther than the "first of all." Instead of the second and the third head-ings that were to mark off the various aspects of his country's glory, came the pitiful question, "What then? are we in worse case than they?"

This shadow that rested over the larger por-tion of the Jewish people was, however, soon to pass away. When the service to which they had been detailed was accomplished, they were to be taken back into oneness with God. "And so," Paul writes, "all Israel shall be saved." [1]

The salvation of Israel was to be accomplished in some way by the aid of the Gentiles. Paul believed that the Jews would be stirred up to jealousy by the acceptance of the Gentiles.[2] Further, it does not appear clearly in what way the fate of the Gentiles was to react on the Jews. Possibly, it was by the direct power of the Gentile church, or of the spirit of God working through it. The complete conversion of the Jews was not, however, to occur until "the fulness of the Gentiles be come in." [3] First, then, all the Gentile world was to be converted and saved. After that the entire Jewish world was to be converted and saved. All this was to happen before the second coming of Christ; and according to the expectation of Paul this second coming was to take place in his own lifetime.

From what has been said it would appear that Paul's doctrine of election is something much less grim and awful than it has generally been supposed, and indeed less so than some of his

[1] Romans xi. 26.   [2] Romans xi. 11.
[3] Romans xi. 25.

words would seem to indicate. The part which one and another was to play in the great consummation had been assigned them. Some had been detailed for the shameful deed of rejecting, or even of crucifying, the Christ of God. They were vessels of dishonor and of wrath. Others had been detailed for the glad and honorable service of welcoming the Christ and building up his kingdom. But in the end all were to be united in one glorious body. "The fulness of the Gentiles" was to be brought in, and "all Israel was to be saved." We have here something of the same nature as the secret decrees of Calvinism ; but the purpose and the result of these decrees are something very different from those of the Calvinistic system. In this latter there were decrees issuing in eternal reprobation. In the thought of Paul they were directions for secret service, in which the sinner and the saint were together working out the great scheme of a final salvation, in which both sinner and saint were to have their part.

From all this Paul would seem to be teaching the doctrine of universal salvation. The results that have been reached are, however, to be taken with certain qualifications. Though Paul has been regarded, and not wholly without right, as the great theologian of the church, yet he was so intensely practical that it is sometimes difficult to get at his full meaning. He seems never to have dwelt upon theory for the sake of theory, or even upon theology for the sake of theology. He was dealing with momentous issues that concerned his readers and himself. He thus fails to give an answer to questions which agitate a more reflective age.

Christ was to appear; the dead in Christ were to arise; but how about those dead who were not in Christ? How about all the past generations of the people of Israel? How about all pre-Christian generations of the Gentile world? Were they to have a share in the great accomplishment? To such questions Paul, at least in his letters that are extant, gives no answer. There is no intimation that they even occurred to him. In the "first Epistle of Peter," we read that Christ "went and preached unto the spirits in prison." [1] Paul may or may not have shared this belief. All that we can say is, that we have no intimation one way or the other.

There is another qualification to be made in

[1] 1 Peter iii. 19.

regard to the apparent universalism of Paul.
He speaks not infrequently as though after all
the result were not so sure as in his lofty moments of enthusiastic confidence he sometimes
states it. He even expresses a fear lest he who
had preached to others should himself be rejected.[1] In the second Epistle to the Thessalonians we have a terrible picture of "the revelation of the Lord Jesus from heaven with the
angels of his power in flaming fire, rendering
vengeance to them that know not God, and to
them that obey not the gospel of our Lord
Jesus : who shall suffer punishment, even eternal destruction from the face of the Lord and
from the glory of his might."[2] In the epistles
that are unquestionably Paul's we find somewhat
similar expressions. Perhaps we ought not to
include among these the stern utterances in the
second chapter of the Epistle to the Romans,
for these were addressed to those who lived under the law. In the first Epistle to the Corinthians, however, he exclaims : "Know ye not
that the unrighteous shall not inherit the kingdom of God?"[3] In the second Epistle to the

---

[1] 1 Corinthians ix. 27.　　　[2] 2 Thessalonians i. 7–9.

[3] 1 Corinthians vi. 9.

Corinthians, he writes : " For we must all be made manifest before the judgement - seat of Christ; that each one may receive the things done in the body, according to what he hath done, whether it be good or bad." [1]

We find thus two forms of speech used by Paul, which seem incompatible. There is the joyous confidence of faith that the fulness of the Gentiles should be brought in, and that all Israel should be saved. So far as the Christians were concerned, he based his confidence upon the fact of their election to salvation. He cries : " If God is for us, who is against us ? . . . Who shall lay anything to the charge of God's elect ? . . . Who shall separate us from the love of Christ ? shall tribulation, or anguish, or persecution, or famine, or nakedness, or peril, or sword ? . . . Nay, in all these things we are more than conquerors through him that loved us. For I am persuaded, that neither death, nor life, nor angels, nor principalities, nor things present, nor things to come, nor powers, nor height, nor depth, nor any other creature, shall be able to separate us from the love of God, which is in Christ Jesus our Lord." [2] On the other hand, we have the

[1] 2 Corinthians v. 10.   [2] Romans viii. 31–39.

fears and the warnings that have been referred
to, — fears lest he who had preached to others
should himself be rejected, — warnings to the
very elect of God against possible sin and condemnation.   All this represents a form of thought
and feeling which is summed up in the "second
Epistle of Peter" in the injunction, "Give the
more diligence to make your calling and election
sure." [1]

If there are these conflicting forms of presentation in regard to the elect, we need not wonder
that the future of men in general is also represented with varying lights and shadows.   In the
one class of expressions Paul spoke as a prophet
to whom the coming glory has been revealed.   In
the other class he spoke as a teacher, warning
as well as encouraging, yet working confidently
towards the accomplishment of the desired result.   Or perhaps this is treating the whole matter too artificially.   Why may we not assume
that Paul, with his fiery temperament, was a man
of moods, and that out of these varying moods
he spoke.

His positive statement is, however, that Jew
and Gentile should alike be gathered in to the

[1] 2 Peter i. 10.

fold of Christ. His warnings and his anxieties do not contradict this; they only make the prophecy less certain. When this result was reached, would come the end.

The Great Consummation.

Upon the scenes that should mark the close of the epic of history Paul does not dwell. He now and then simply indicates the sublimity of this consummation. To the Thessalonians he writes: "For the Lord himself shall descend from heaven, with a shout, with the voice of the archangel, and with the trump of God: and the dead in Christ shall rise first: then we that are alive, that are left, shall together with them be caught up in the clouds, to meet the Lord in the air: and so shall we ever be with the Lord." [1] Later, to the Corinthians he wrote: "We shall not all sleep, but we shall all be changed, in a moment, in the twinkling of an eye, at the last trump: for the trumpet shall sound, and the dead shall be raised incorruptible, and we shall be changed." [2] Only one brief hint does Paul give of the " new heaven " and the " new earth " [3] of

[1] 1 Thessalonians iv. 16.
[2] 1 Corinthians xv. 51, 52.　　　[3] Revelation xxi. 1.

which we read in the book of the Revelation.
To the Romans he wrote : " For we know that
the whole creation groaneth and travaileth in
pain together until now." [1]   This would seem to
imply that Paul held the belief, common to the
Jewish teachers of his time, that at the coming
of the Messiah the earth itself should be re-
newed.[2]

In all this Christ had been the great accom-
plisher. All things had been put under him,
that he might fulfil the work of the Messiah.
" But," says Paul, " when he saith, All things are
put in subjection, it is evident that he is excepted
who did subject all things unto him. And when
all things have been subjected unto him, then
shall the Son also himself be subjected to him
that did subject all things unto him, that God
may be all in all." [3]   It would seem as if this
single verse should have stood in the way of
the ascription of Deity to Jesus. No exaltation of Jesus short of the Godhead is too great
for Paul, but at this he paused. Later ages have
been carried on by the impulse received from

---

[1] Romans viii. 22.

[2] Weber's *System der Palästinischen Theologie*, pp. 380 ff.

[3] 1 Corinthians xv. 27 f.

him, when they have passed the sacred limits where Paul rested ; but in naming Jesus God they contradict his teaching. In the last glimpse that Paul gives us of the glorified Christ, his special work has been accomplished. His regency is at an end. He takes his place with the world that he has redeemed. This is all that we see of the great consummation. All else is lost in the glory of the God who is "all in all."

CHAPTER VI.

PAUL'S DOCTRINE OF SALVATION.

WE have thus considered Paul's teaching in regard to the abolition of the law and in regard to the remission of sins. We have glanced at his philosophy of history. The central and essential element of his teaching has, however, not yet been touched upon by us. This central and essential element is his doctrine of salvation. The abolition of the law and the remission of the sins that had been committed against it formed, in the thought of Paul, only the introduction to the real substance of the work of Christ. They were the negative aspect of this work. Paul's doctrine of salvation presents what was, in his view, the positive aspect of the work of Christ. How completely the doctrine of the atonement by the death of Christ belonged to the negative and preparatory part of his work may be illustrated by a remark by Professor Pfleiderer in a paper of comparatively early date. Professor Pfleiderer said : " Paul refers to atonement by the death of

Christ only in relation to Judaizers ; not once in regard to the spiritual life."[1]

With the abolition of the law and the remission of sins the old epoch closed and the field was left open to the new. When Paul says, "Our old man was crucified with him,"[2] he implies the sweeping away by the death of Christ of old associations and conditions. The former man was a slave to the law and was tainted with sin ; the new man is free and filled with the spirit of God. It is the constitution of this new man which we have now briefly to consider.

I wish to emphasize the fact that under this heading is included the positive and substantial teaching of Paul, because the little space which is here given to the discussion of this might seem to imply a lack of appreciation of its importance. The special object of this book has been, however, to state and illustrate what I conceive to be the real significance of Paul's teaching in regard to the Jewish law and to the atonement. If I have referred to other aspects of Paul's teaching it is because they illustrate this or are illustrated by it. I here refer to

[1] *Zeitschrift für Wissenschaftliche Theologie*, xv. 195.
[2] Romans vi. 6.

Paul's doctrine of salvation chiefly to indicate what a small place the theory of the atonement filled in his general scheme. If he devoted the Epistle to the Galatians to it, it was because the Galatians were being misled by false teachers. In the Epistle to the Romans the various elements of his system are exhibited in their due proportion. The atonement that was accomplished by the crucifixion of Christ touched the Christian life only at its beginning, except that the moral influence of the event and the grateful love which was called out by it were perpetual factors in the Christian's experience.

While the higher life of the new dispensation is, on the whole, clearly stated, there are certain points which to me at least are obscure, and in regard to which I fail to obtain much light from those from whom I have sought it. This difference in the clearness of the statements in regard to the two aspects of Paul's teaching is not unnatural. In the one case we have to do with logic ; in the other with insight. When an argument is wrought out with any approach to logical consistency, it ought not to be difficult to reach its meaning. In what I have called an insight, on the contrary, the elements are not analyzed. The result is presented as a whole, and the perfect comprehension of it depends upon habits and conditions of thought and feeling, preconceived notions, and half‑conscious assumptions, which may be in part or wholly unknown to us.

One of the questions to which it is sometimes difficult to give a perfectly satisfactory answer is that in regard to the identification of the Christian with his Lord. This identification is continually referred to. Paul exclaims : " I live ; and yet no longer I, but Christ liveth in me." [1] The Christians are told that they are " the body of Christ." [2] It is, indeed, needless to multiply such illustrations. It is an interesting question whether forms of speech like those that I have cited are used in a literal, mystical sense; or whether they are used figuratively. According to one view, when, for instance, Paul says that it is Christ that liveth in him, he meant that he was united to the risen Christ in a mystical union, so that his own separate individuality was lost, and it was no more he that lived but Christ that lived in him. If the other interpretation be adopted, Paul would mean that he had submitted

[1] Galatians ii. 20.   [2] 1 Corinthians xii. 27.

himself so thoroughly to the influence of Jesus that it was as if Jesus lived in him. I do not know of any criterion by which we can absolutely determine, in many cases, which interpretation is the true one.

If we decide, in regard to any of these cases, in favor of the mystical interpretation, another question is forced upon us to which it is equally difficult to give an explicit answer. The question is, What was, in the thought of Paul, the relation between the indwelling Christ and the indwelling Spirit ? The same forms of speech are used in regard to both relations, that of the soul to Christ and that of the soul to the divine Spirit. This similarity of usage may help us understand how it happened that among the early Christians the view was more or less prevalent that the Logos and the Holy Ghost were one and the same. This view might seem, further, to have a verbal support in the saying of Paul, " Now the Lord is the Spirit." [1]

In the book of Acts there is evidently a difference in time between the conversion of the believer to Christ and the reception by him of the Holy Ghost. Perhaps, however, we have no right

[1] 2 Corinthians iii. 17.

to let this fact influence our judgment of the thought of Paul. In one passage Paul at least appears to make a distinction between the two. "Ye are not," he says, "in the flesh, but in the spirit, if so be that the Spirit of God dwelleth in you. But if any man hath not the Spirit of Christ, he is none of his. And if Christ is in you, the body is dead because of sin ; but the spirit is life because of righteousness. But if the Spirit of him that raised up Jesus from the dead dwelleth in you, he that raised up Christ Jesus from the dead shall quicken also your mortal bodies through his Spirit that dwelleth in you." [1] If we could fully understand this passage we should thoroughly comprehend the positive doctrine of Paul. In some parts of it the two elements of the higher life would seem to be the same ; in others they would seem to be different. If they are the same, how can we avoid the ancient doctrine just referred to of the identity of the Logos and the Holy Ghost ? If they are different, what is the nature of the difference ?

Perhaps the difficulty is theoretical rather than practical. Perhaps we may regard Paul's doctrine of the Holy Spirit as furnishing its solu-

[1] Romans viii. 9 ff.

tion. It may be that in the thought of Paul it
was by the power of the Holy Ghost that Christ
and his followers were taken out of their sepa-
rateness and made one. It may be that the Holy
Ghost in this manner formed the uniting and
inspiring life of the body of Christ.

Whatever difficulties the details of Paul's system may occasion, there is no doubt in regard
to the general substance of his thought. The
work of Christ, in itself and in connection with
the work of the Spirit which came through him,
was accomplished in two ways, or consisted of
two elements. The one, in the lack of a better
term, we may call mystical; the other we may
call moral. The former of these elements was
the indwelling of the Spirit of God in the believer; with which, if we take the expressions
referred to above in the literal sense, we must
associate the indwelling Christ. This indwelling life of the Spirit worked both negatively and
positively. Its negative work had to do with
the sinfulness of the flesh which was inherited
from Adam. There was, through Jesus, introduced into the system a power which penetrated
it in every part, which met and contended with
and expelled the virus of sin. This is in part

what Paul meant by the condemning of sin in
the flesh.[1] The result of this was twofold. It
enabled the Christian to lead a holy life. Further, since death came through sin, the cleansing
of the flesh from the virus of sin took it out
from the dominion of death, so that at the coming of Christ the dead in Christ should be raised,
and those who were alive should become changed
without going through the form of death. The
positive side of this mystical element in the
work of Christ was the indwelling of the Holy
Ghost, and, if we accept the literal interpretation of Paul's words, the indwelling of Christ,
as an actual life. We recognize two forms of
the positive activity of the Holy Ghost. These
we may call by an inaccurate use of terms the
supernatural and the natural; or we may speak
of them, more truly, as the special and the universal or normal. According to the former,
that which I have called the supernatural or the
special, the Holy Spirit assumed control of the
finite spirit as an invading force. In this manner came the various gifts of the Spirit, the
gift of tongues and the like. Paul's more ordi-

[1] Romans viii. 3. " He made sin forfeit its dominion."
Meyer, a. l.

nary manner of speech refers, however, to what
I have called the natural, universal, or normal
form of the Spirit's working. In this the Divine
Spirit became blended with the human spirit, as
the life of a tree becomes blended with that of
the leaf so that it is not to be distinguished from
it. Thus, in the Epistle to the Philippians we
have the paradoxical injunction, " Work out your
own salvation with fear and trembling ; for it is
God which worketh in you both to will and to
work, for his good pleasure." [1] Here we see how
the divine and the human are absolutely blended
in the process so that even the very willing is of
God. Elsewhere we are told that " the fruit
of the Spirit is love, joy, peace, longsuffering,
kindness, goodness, faithfulness, meekness, tem-
perance." [2] These fruits of the Spirit are of no
foreign growth. They are the natural products
of the life of the soul. The Divine Spirit, rein-
forcing the life and working in and through it,
simply brings them to fairer results and fuller
proportions. It is for this reason that I have
called this the natural operation of the Spirit in
contrast with that form of its working which
breaks in upon and suspends or transforms the

[1] Philippians ii. 12 f.   [2] Galatians v. 22 f.

ordinary functions of the spiritual life. I have called it also universal and normal, because it belongs to no special crisis of the world's history, but represents the normal and general relation of the soul to God.

The other element in the work of Christ I have called the moral element. I here refer to the spiritual activity which is carried on in the full light of consciousness. It works by means of influences that act upon the soul by appealing to its better life, placing before it motives which stimulate and ideals which guide its development. A great, perhaps the greatest, factor in this open and recognized influence was for Paul the personality of Christ. The epistles of Paul are full of references to this. "Be ye imitators of me," he says to the Corinthians, "even as I also am of Christ." [1] Elsewhere he says to the same people : "But we all, with unveiled face reflecting as a mirror the glory of the Lord, are transformed into the same image from glory to glory, even as from the Lord the Spirit." [2] To urge the personality of Christ upon his followers and to realize it for himself, Paul did not need to dwell much upon the facts of Christ's

---

[1] 1 Corinthians xi. 1   [2] 2 Corinthians iii. 18.

personal history upon the earth. The self-sacrificing love of Christ was for him summed up in the contrast between the heavenly glory which he had left and the lowliness of the life of service which he had chosen. This life found its culmination and symbol in the painful and shameful death of the cross, by means of which the end that had been the impulse to this degradation was accomplished.

We have already referred to the difficulty of determining, in all cases, what phrases of Paul are used in a mystical and what in a moral sense. With regard to many of Paul's expressions, however, there can be no doubt that they are used in a symbolical or moral sense. Thus when he speaks of being buried with Christ in baptism and rising to newness of life,[1] there can be little doubt that the phraseology is symbolical. This passage, it should be noticed, refers to no conception of Paul differing from the views elsewhere expressed by him in regard to the atonement. The two forms of expression simply represent opposite aspects, the positive and the negative, of the same transaction.

To Paul, Jesus represented the highest ideal

[1] Romans vi. 4.

of life. To this ideal he was drawn by reverence
and love and gratitude. He felt that he owed
everything to him; and he felt that Jesus was
worthy of the offering of his whole life. The
thought of Jesus represented the sphere in
which he lived and the inspiration and goal of
his living. In his language, indeed, all aglow
as it was with the fervor of his spirit, it is difficult sometimes to distinguish whether the person of Christ or the teaching of Christ is referred to. To Paul we may imagine there was
little difference between the two. The person
and the work of Christ were so fused together
that they were one. It was the work which
manifested the person and served as its instrument; and the person was revealed only in and
through the work. As for Paul himself, he had
no life apart from that which he led in and
through and for his Lord.

If we leave out of the account the relations
that we have been considering, Paul's doctrine
of liberty would be wholly misunderstood. Apart
from these, liberty would be merely license. It
is to be noticed that Paul nowhere intimates that
the law had been annulled. It was the voice of
the law itself which condemned the Christian,

because he was a Christian, to that outlawry
which was to him liberty and a new life. For
those who were not Christians it made its old
demands and uttered its old thunders. For those
who were Christians it stood ready to lay hold of
them again in case they relapsed from their allegiance to Christ. The two, Christ and the law,
stood before men, and one or the other claimed
their allegiance. They could not serve both.
Paul wrote to the Galatians: "Yea, I testify
again to every man that receiveth circumcision,
that he is a debtor to do the whole law. Ye are
severed from Christ, ye who would be justified
by the law."[1] To Paul's thought no one was
made free of the law through Christ who did not
stand to Christ in such an intimate relation of
faith and love and acceptance that he shared
with him the legal pollution of his crucifixion.[2]
One who was so united with Christ must of necessity feel the power of his personality, and
must receive those spiritual gifts which came
through Christ. Thus only those were free of

[1] Galatians v. 3, 4.

[2] "In his" (Paul's) "view, deadness to the law, the result of
faith in Christ, was also deadness to sin." Toy's *Judaism and
Christianity*, p. 209.

the law who were taken up into the higher life of Christian love and inspiration.

This higher life of the spirit is what Paul was aiming at in all his writing and preaching. How closely he had this at heart is seen from those injunctions, so inspiring and tender, so full of human insight and of moral strength, which now and then interrupt his closer thought, and which crown the close of every epistle. In these we learn to love the man, as in his strength and courage we had learned to admire him.

CONCLUSION.

THE interpretation which I have presented of Paul's doctrine of the atonement appears to me to be so clearly taught by him that I cannot help believing that it will become at some time the generally accepted view of his teaching. I cannot hope that it will, to any very great extent, become at once so accepted. The associations with the phraseology of Paul are so strong that it is probable that they will, for a time, hold their own, in spite of the distinctness with which Paul says something which these associations wholly misrepresent. Still, it is worth while to ask what will be the effect upon religious thought and feeling when this view of Paul's teaching shall become accepted ; and also what is the general interest that should attach itself to this discussion.

To those who take the same view of the Jewish law that Paul did, that is, to those who accept it as the supernaturally given ordinance of God, Paul's reasoning will hold in the same sense that it had for him and his followers. They will feel that they are freed from the law by the fact that Jesus bore its curse, and that he shed his blood for the remission of their sins.

For those who do not have this belief in the divine authority of the Jewish law, or who have not so vivid a sense of this authority, the cross of Christ will still remain the instrument by which Christianity gained possession of the world. The crucifixion will be of interest, not merely as any other martyrdom, but because it was precisely by this form of death that Christ won the victory which brought his gospel to the Gentile world. Thus the cross will still remain the symbol of victory through shame, and will still be seen to be the source of spiritual life to the world. It will thus remain the sign by which the victory over the powers of evil is to be accomplished.

If we look at other than the strictly religious aspect of the result, we shall still find it full of interest. It presents in a new light the magnificent figure of Paul. Perhaps we may feel the power of his genius more than it could have been felt under the shadow of the awful and mysterious doctrines that have been associated

with his name.   Certainly the power of his personality will be felt more clearly.   The two parts
of his life will be seen to fit together as they
could not have been seen to do before.   We see
in Paul a man of fiery emotions, whose emotions
were wholly under the guidance of his intellect.
Perhaps there was never a man of so passionate
a nature who was so absolutely controlled by his
reason.   This control is shown not merely by a
life dominated by an idea.   Such lives are not
rare.   The control is shown by the sudden and
absolute change of life at the command of his
reason, which first demanded one form of life
and then under the guidance of an inflexible
logic demanded another.

There was, perhaps, never another instance of
so complete a change as Paul underwent, occurring as it did in the case of Paul without foreign
impulse.   The inspiration came, indeed, from
Jesus ; but the form which its working took was
wholly peculiar to Paul.   The change was not
merely in regard to outward observances.   It affected the inmost sources and methods of his
life.   We are in the habit of looking upon the
Jewish law chiefly with reference to its ritual,
using this word in its widest sense.   To Paul

and to Jesus the law was primarily something very different from this. To them love was "the fulfilment of the law." [1] They regarded the law, therefore, as primarily referring, in the expression of Jesus, to love to God and man.[2] In the law that, according to the thought of Paul, was abolished for the Christian by the death of Christ was included the spiritual and moral as well as the ceremonial law. Of this Paul's language leaves no doubt. He says, for instance: "What then? shall we sin, because we are not under law, but under grace?" [3] In another place, he says: "For ye, brethren, were called for freedom; only use not your freedom for an occasion for the flesh." [4] These sayings and others which might be quoted make it perfectly clear that freedom with Paul was freedom from every positive command. Life was henceforth to be based not on external authority, but upon the impulses of a heart transformed by the power of Jesus and of the Holy Ghost. With this change of mental attitude the entire spirit of Paul seems to have been changed. Before, he had been the narrow and hard persecutor.

---

[1] Romans xiii. 10.
[2] Matthew xxii. 37–39.
[3] Romans vi. 15.
[4] Galatians v. 13.

Now all the beauty of his nature blossomed in the genial light of the new truth. He becomes the ideal of breadth and of tender sympathy. It is interesting to see how he anticipates what is most marked in our modern ethics. When he speaks of the Christians as being "members one of another,"[1] and remember that with him Christianity was to embrace the world, we find an anticipation of that recognition of the solidarity of society which is becoming more and more the foundation of our ethics ; while the exclamation, "If any will not work, neither let him eat,"[2] which anticipates our whole idea of charity, sounds so much like Paul that I am unwilling to doubt its genuineness.

The expressions which to many have made Paul appear hard and dogmatic are merely expressions of the largeness of his nature. In the passage which has suggested the title of this book, Paul exclaims, "But though we, or an angel from heaven, should preach unto you any gospel other than that which we preached unto

[1] This expression from Ephesians iv. 25, simply sums up forms of speech common in his unquestioned epistles. Compare 1 Corinthians xii. 26, *et passim.*

[2] 2 Thessalonians iii. 10.

you, let him be anathema." [1] What could seem more narrow and bigoted than this? When we ask, however, what was the gospel of which Paul speaks, the nature of these words is changed. The whole tenor of the epistle from which these words are taken show that the gospel to which he refers is the gospel of freedom. It was a gospel that had struck off the chains from the human spirit; and Paul cries, "Though we or an angel from heaven should seek to bind again the follower of Christ, let him be anathema." What seems an outburst of dogmatism is a protest against dogmatism. So far as the aspect of his gospel to which reference is here made is concerned, the most advanced and freest thinker of our own day could say Amen.

Another illustration of Paul's greatness is found in his attitude toward the law which he discarded. He does not turn against it with scorn and hate. He still believes it to have been God's law. He would not have passed beyond it except at its own bidding. Wholly characteristic of his conservatism in the midst of the radical transformation which he was accomplishing is the phrase which has been so often quoted

[1] Galatians i. 8.

on these pages, "I *through the law* died unto the law." [1] Only through the law would Paul have been willing to die to it.

We feel the greatness of Paul all the more when we consider the work which he accomplished. It was he who gave Christianity to the world. We owe it to him that Christianity did not continue as a Jewish sect, unless indeed it had perished as such. It is idle, indeed, to say in regard to the course of history what might have been if something that was had not been. It is not idle, however, to say that, so far as the reality of history is concerned, the world owes Christianity to Paul. When we think what Europe and America would have been and would be without Christianity, what the life of the individual, what the social order, what painting and music and architecture would have been without it ; we can faintly realize the extent of the world's indebtedness to Paul. Surely no question of history could be more interesting or important than the one that we have been considering, namely, how this movement by which Christianity passed from the condition of a Jewish sect to that of a world religion was accom-

[1] Galatians ii. 19.

plished. It is a question which is as interesting
from the historical as from the theological point
of view. When we look closely at the matter,
as we have done, we find it even more interesting than we might have expected. The dialectic
of Paul, by which the law was the agent of its
own overthrow, amazes us. If this were a bit
of legal strategy we should admire its audacity.
It is more to be admired when we see in it the
natural working of an earnest mind which, by its
very reverence for the law, was emancipated from
the law.

The transaction gains in interest when we
observe how little change the teachings of Jesus
undergo, when, by this dialectic of Paul, they
cease to be provincial and become universal.
Paul's legality concerned only the law. The law
contained, so to speak, two elements which were
brought to bear on one another in such a manner that the law itself became dissolved as in a
vapor and passed away. The shock of the change
left the teaching of Jesus as it was before. Under the interpretation of Paul's teaching that
has for centuries been prevalent in the church,
this was not the case. The doctrine which made
the divine forgiveness impossible without an

infinite sacrifice for sin obliged the Christian
to take the sermon on the mount, the parable of
the prodigal son, the Lord's prayer, and much
of Christ's other teaching, with many qualifications. The parable of the prodigal son could not
represent the return of the sinner to God, for
the prodigal was received by a waiting love
which demanded no vicarious suffering. When
Paul is rightly understood, this parable and the
other sayings to which I have referred may be
taken in the simple beauty of their natural
meaning.

We see, also, how Paul's teaching, rightly
understood, leaves undisturbed our confidence in
human nature. Paul taught, indeed, the depravity of the flesh derived from Adam's sin. "They
that are in the flesh," he tells us, "cannot please
God." [1] This doctrine of inherited sin, however,
was not a part of Paul's original thought. He
was confronted by this doctrine of the Jewish
teachers as he was confronted by the barrier of
the law. As his dialectic abolished the law, so
that it was to the Christian as if it had never
been ; so his doctrine of the power of Christ and
of the Holy Spirit abolished this taint of inherited

[1] Romans viii. 8.

sin, and the spirit and the flesh were left free to
become the temple of God. Here, again, what
seems Paul's narrowness is the negation of narrowness. It was the natural method by which
the teaching of Jesus was set free from local
forms of thought, so that it could appeal to the
universal consciousness of man.

There are other elements of Paul's teaching,
however, which introduce new elements, if not
into the teaching of Christ at least into the conception of the person of Christ. Christ was,
indeed, to him never God. The church in the
deification of Christ has followed the momentum
derived from Paul, but has been carried by it far
beyond the point which he himself had reached.
Though, however, Paul did not exalt Christ to
the deity, he did invest him with a superhuman
and preëxistent glory by which he stood beneath
God alone. There is, however, a vast difference
between this exaltation of Christ and a transformation of his teaching which beclouds his
thought and is out of harmony with man's developed sense of justice. It is not to my purpose
to discuss the question how far this exaltation
of Jesus was peculiar to Paul, and how far it
was shared with the non-Pauline church, or how

far the doctrine of the speedy return of Christ
to judge the world was derived from the words
of Jesus rightly or wrongly understood. This
exaltation added simply a framework to Christianity which did not affect its moral aspect.
What I wish to emphasize in these closing
words is the manner in which the teaching of
Jesus was, by the dialectic of Paul, transferred
without substantial change to world-wide influence.

INDEX

OF

CITATIONS FROM THE BIBLE.

Poetry, Comedy, and Duty.

BY

CHARLES CARROLL EVERETT, D. D.

Professor of Theology in the Divinity School of Harvard University.

Crown 8vo, pp. 315, gilt top, $1.50.

*I. Poetry : The Imagination ; The Philosophy of Poetry ;
The Poetic Aspect of Nature ; The Tragic Forces in
Life and Literature. II. Comedy : The Philosophy of
the Comic. III. The Ultimate Facts of Ethics ; The
New Ethics. IV. Conclusion : Poetry, Comedy, and
Duty, considered in their relation to one another.*

In this work Poetry, taken as representing the
æsthetic side of life, Comedy, and Duty are regarded as making up our relation to the environment ideally considered. They are first treated
separately, and then their relation to one another
is considered.

An abstract discussion of the æsthetic and ethical
elements in the mind is a rare contribution to ethical
literature, and one in which the logical element is so
vigorous, the illustration so ample and apt, and the
scope so broad, as is the case with this volume, is a
treasure-trove. — *The Atlantic Monthly.*

It is necessary only to notice the author's clear and
precise method of developing his subject, the absence
of all controversy from his manner, the extreme con-
scientiousness of his thinking, which are distinguishing qualities of his work. . . . Those who are skilled
to think and write like this are few in our day. — *The
Nation (New York).*

A book so sagely optimistic in tone, so lofty in its
conceptions, so stimulating in argument, that it cannot
fail to benefit the mind with which it comes in contact.
— *The Literary World (Boston).*

*For sale by all Booksellers. Sent by mail, post-paid, on receipt of
price by the Publishers,*

HOUGHTON, MIFFLIN AND COMPANY,

4 PARK ST., BOSTON; 11 EAST 17TH ST., NEW YORK.

The Science of Thought.

BY

CHARLES CARROLL EVERETT.

Revised Edition.   Pp. 430, $1.50.

It is the aim of this work to consider thought as a reality, to approach it as any work of true science approaches its material.   It first discusses the relations that make up the substance of actual thought.   It then analyzes thought into its elements and follows it into its fundamental divisions.   It shows the method of each of these, the kind of argument, and the degree of certainty of which it admits.   Especially does it seek to present in the ideas of the reason the principles which the mind accepts as its final test of truth.

" The Science of Thought " is the nearest approach to the lines along which life moves.   It is the logic which my interpretation of history and my own philosophy rest upon, and is therefore the logic for my classes. — H. H. WILLIAMS, *Professor of Philosophy in the University of North Carolina.*

It would be hard to name any other book America has produced which would so deepen the reason of its serious reader. — Rev. FRANCIS TIFFANY, in *Christian Register.*

Published by

DeWOLFE, FISKE AND COMPANY,

BOSTON.